At Home
in the Vineyard

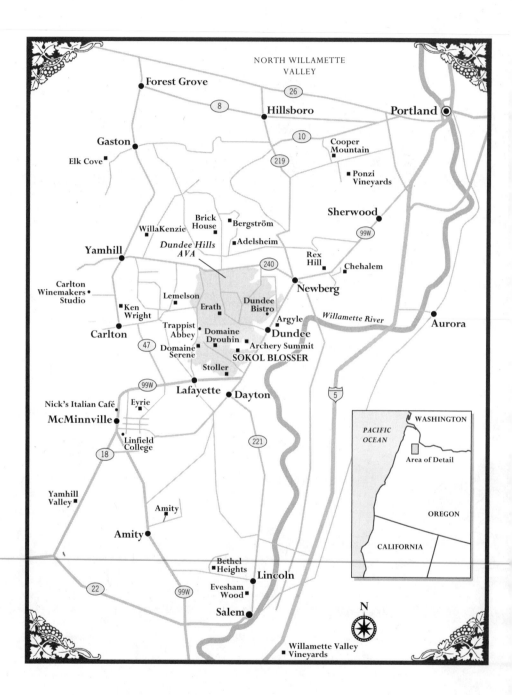

NORTH WILLAMETTE
VALLEY

Forest Grove

26

8   Hillsboro   Portland ⊙

Gaston   10

Cooper
Mountain

Elk Cove ■   219

■ Ponzi
Vineyards

Brick   Sherwood
House   ■ Bergström
WillaKenzie ■   99W
Yamhill   *Dundee Hills*
AVA   ■ Adelsheim

Carlton   Rex
Winemakers •   Lemelson   Hill   ■ Chehalem
Studio   ■   240
■ Ken   Erath   Dundee   Newberg
Wright   Bistro
Trappist   ■ Argyle *Willamette River*   Aurora
Carlton   Abbey   ■ Domaine   ● Dundee
47   Drouhin
■ Domaine   ■ Archery Summit
Serene   SOKOL BLOSSER
■ Stoller

99W   Lafayette ● Dayton   5

Nick's Italian Café ■   221
■ Eyrie
McMinnville ●
■ Linfield
College
18

Yamhill
Valley ■
■ Amity

Amity ●

Bethel
■ Heights   Lincoln
22   99W   Evesham
Wood ■
Salem ●

N

Willamette Valley
■ Vineyards

PACIFIC   WASHINGTON
OCEAN

Area of Detail

OREGON

CALIFORNIA

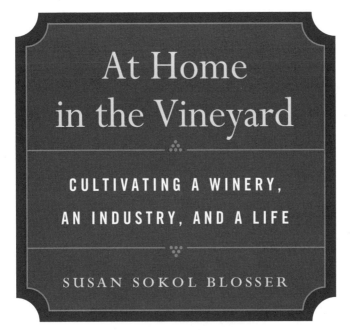

At Home in the Vineyard

CULTIVATING A WINERY, AN INDUSTRY, AND A LIFE

SUSAN SOKOL BLOSSER

UNIVERSITY OF CALIFORNIA PRESS

Berkeley   Los Angeles   London

University of California Press, one of the most
distinguished university presses in the United States, enriches
lives around the world by advancing scholarship in the humanities,
social sciences, and natural sciences. Its activities are supported by the
UC Press Foundation and by philanthropic contributions from
individuals and institutions. For more information,
visit www.ucpress.edu.

Unless otherwise noted, all photos are from the Sokol Blosser family.
Map by James Sinclair.

University of California Press
Berkeley and Los Angeles, California

University of California Press, Ltd.
London, England

Library of Congress Cataloging-in-Publication Data
Blosser, Susan Sokol.
At home in the vineyard : cultivating a wintery,
an industry, and a life / Susan Sokol Blosser.
p.   cm.
Includes index.
ISBN 978-0-520-25629-3 (pbk : alk.)
1. Blosser, Susan Sokol.   2. Vintners—Oregon—
Biography.   3. Wine and wine making—Oregon.   4. Wine
industry—Oregon.   I. Title.
TP547.B56A3   2006
663'.20092—dc22   2005033824

Manufactured in the United States of America
17 16 15 14 13 12 11 10 09 08
12 11 10 9 8 7 6 5 4 3 2 1

To Bill, who started the grand adventure
To Nik, Alex, and Alison, who enriched it beyond words
And to Russ, who took it to the next level

CONTENTS

ILLUSTRATIONS

Photographs

Graphs

ACKNOWLEDGMENTS

I wanted to write this book myself. I was adamant about not having a ghost-writer put my story into words for me. This made the creation process longer and more arduous than it would otherwise have been, but also more satisfying. While I take full responsibility for the finished manuscript, like every author I am grateful to the friends and family who encouraged me and took time to read the manuscript. Special thanks to Emily Crumpacker and Norma Paulus, who got me started; to Nancy Wolfson, Brian Doyle, and Marianne Keddington-Lang, who offered valuable literary advice; to Dave Adelsheim and Eugenia Keegan, who helped me go back in time and pinpoint dates and issues; and to Heidi Yorkshire, a writer and author herself, who showed true friendship with her ruthless critiques, gently given. Bill Blosser and our children, Nik, Alex, and Alison, cheered me all the way. Russ Rosner came to my aid on all fronts. And at the end, when I felt I'd gone as far as I could go, Suzan Hall's help and suggestions carried me home.

A heartfelt thank-you to all.

Susan Sokol Blosser
Dundee, Oregon
2006

———— ·•· ————

Germination

I set out to write a history of the Oregon wine industry, but I realized that the only story I could tell was my own. That story, my story, is tightly interwoven with two others: the wine industry's growth and Sokol Blosser Winery's creation. While I was writing, I kept asking myself, "Is this going to be a wine book, a business book, or a memoir?" As the story unfolded, I knew it had to be all three. The strands create a multitextured tapestry, sometimes coarse-grained and gritty, occasionally gossamer and luminescent. It is woven in earth tones—the sturdy brown-red of the soil in the Dundee Hills of northwestern Oregon; the translucent yellow-green of young grape leaves; streaks of cerulean from the bluebirds zipping around the vines; the deeper green of the mature vine canopy; and the miraculous transformation of Pinot Noir clusters from green to red to purple, one grape at a time. Look closely, and you well may see tearstains. Tears of joy, or of sorrow? I will tell you now, there were a lot of each.

In the early 1970s, when my husband, Bill Blosser, and I started our vineyard, we were young, energetic, brash, and looking for the meaning of life. I had a bachelor's degree from Stanford University and a master of arts in teaching from Reed College. I had pursued a top-notch education because I liked school and had been told early on that I had a responsibility to use the brain I had been given. Married two months after college graduation, I did what most women of my generation did: I followed my husband.

Flash forward some thirty years. The University of Portland has awarded me an honorary doctorate of public service, citing my business entrepreneurship, commitment to sustainability, and community service. How did that young woman with no clear direction or special skills turn into a seasoned business owner whom a university would choose to honor?

This book chronicles that transformation as well as the emergence and development of the wine industry in Oregon and the growth of Sokol Blosser Winery. Wine book, business book, memoir. The picture is layered and complex.

The vineyard that began as the whim of two young idealists, Bill Blosser and me, turned into something larger and more interesting than I could ever have imagined. Over the years, as we maneuvered past the obstacles, significant things happened. Life surprised us. We matured and changed, Sokol Blosser Winery grew and flourished, and the fledgling Oregon wine industry took its place on the world stage.

Life has been good. Not easy, but good. This is how it looked and felt to me.

I

Roots

In the last two weeks of 1970, Bill and I each gave birth. I had our first child, Nik, and Bill closed the deal on our first piece of vineyard land. We had no idea, then, how dramatically the arrival of those two babies would change the direction of our lives.

We were in our mid-twenties, had been married four years, and had spent most of that time in graduate school, first in Oregon for my master of arts in teaching from Reed College and then in North Carolina for Bill's master of city and regional planning from Chapel Hill. We had studied hard and played hard. Our 1968 Volkswagen camper bus, a miniature house on wheels, had carried us all over the continent. We hiked and picked wild huckleberries in the Mount Adams Wilderness in Washington State. We camped near Old Faithful and fled, early the next morning, singing loudly to scare off a nosy grizzly bear. We drove to Lake Louise and across the wheat-colored plains of Saskatchewan, fighting headwinds that held our boxy vehicle under forty miles per hour. We explored the entire Blue Ridge Parkway, sleeping in the bus and cooking over campfires, stopping only for supplies and a new block of ice for our tiny refrigerator. With no kids, no pets, no house to worry about, we never hesitated when another trip beckoned.

Summers in Chapel Hill, we played tennis every evening, waiting for the muggy heat to retreat before we went out. Winters, we tried out complicated recipes from Julia Child's new cookbooks and discussed politics, civil rights, and feminism with the other student couples, mostly North-erners like us who were fascinated with southern living. We protested the Vietnam War and drove to Washington, D.C., with friends to join the candle-light vigils and marches.

When the baby and the vineyard arrived, life abruptly changed course. Road trips, camping and hiking, tennis after dinner, spontaneous parties—all these became memories.

Baby Nik actually had a longer gestation period than Bill's land pur-chase. The idea of a vineyard seemed to arrive out of nowhere, a bit of whimsy that took on a life of its own. We were on our way from Chapel Hill back to Oregon, where Bill was to teach urban planning at Portland State University. Near Lancaster, Pennsylvania, we stopped to browse at a flea market. It was Pennsylvania Dutch country, and we thought we might find something old and wonderful hidden in the junk. We meandered through with the other bargain hunters, and somewhere in the midst of the tables laden with wooden clocks, rusty fruit bins, and old kitchen utensils, the idea of a vineyard popped into Bill's head.

"What do you think about growing grapes?" he asked, as we bent over a particularly handsome mantel clock.

"Grow grapes?" I asked. "You mean to make wine?" Where had that come from? What was going on in his head? I gaped at him.

"Why not? I think it would be a neat thing to do."

We lost interest in the mantel clock and headed back to our camper. All the way back to Oregon, this outlandish idea kept coming up. The more we talked about it, the more interesting it became.

We both liked wine. Bill had spent a year in France during college, tak-ing classes in Paris and then working as a dishwasher at a mountain resort near Grenoble. He had emerged from that experience a wine-drinking, French-speaking Francophile, with a worldliness that had attracted me to him in college. I had spent the summer after high school studying in France, and I had grown up drinking wine, especially Bordeaux and Burgundy. Collecting wine was my father's hobby, and he had taken time to educate me about the contents of the large cellar he had created in our basement.

True, Bill and I had no experience with the production side, but we liked the idea of going back to the land and growing something that made life more enjoyable. We would never have been attracted to soybeans or corn, but growing wine grapes had both aesthetic and emotional appeal. Wine symbolized culture and sophistication. People had been making wine for centuries—how hard could it be?

In Portland, we found a house to rent and began researching the geography, soils, and climate that wine grapes required. We knew about the wine industry in Napa; we had celebrated our engagement at a picnic on the grounds of Beringer Winery in 1966. But Napa seemed crowded and expensive even then. Other parts of Northern California were more interesting. On a visit to Bill's folks in Oakland, we scouted for possible vineyard sites around Ukiah and Mendocino, where Bill's family had homesteaded in the 1850s. When we saw a magazine article about another city-planning graduate, Tony Husch, who had started a vineyard near Philo in Mendocino, we took it as a sign to keep going.

We didn't know there were already people growing grapes in Oregon until, driving through the countryside one Saturday, we stopped at a one-room real estate office in Newberg to inquire about land. It was useless to ask directly about vineyard land back then, because real estate agents had no idea what that meant. Bill was describing the kind of land he was looking for, in terms of slope and exposure and soils, when the agent said, "See that guy over there, looking at the book of listings? He just asked me the same question."

Bill introduced himself to Gary Fuqua, who had driven down from Seattle. The real estate agent, shaking his head at what people would think up, tried to help. "Have you talked to the guy up on Kings Grade Road?" he asked. "A big, friendly guy. He has just planted a vineyard and seems to know what he's talking about." Following the agent's directions, we found the ramshackle house where Dick Erath, his wife, Kina, and their two toddler sons were living. Dick had bought the property and planted vines in 1968.

But Dick and Kina had not been the first, either. Two other couples, the Courys and the Letts, had bought land in the Willamette Valley a few years earlier. David Lett and Chuck Coury had met in the early 1960s, when they were both studying enology and viticulture at the University of California, Davis. Chuck wrote his master's thesis on the climate-grape connection between Burgundy and Oregon, concluding that the highest-quality wines would be produced in areas in which grape maturation coincided with the end of the growing season. If the climate were too warm, he argued, grapes would not develop complex flavors, because they would get sweet, or ripen, before they matured. The search for a climate that would meet the simultaneous maturation-ripening parameters for growing Pinot Noir, Chardonnay, and Riesling—the grapes that interested him—led him to Oregon. Coury's theory made sense to Lett, so he and his wife, Diana, spent their honeymoon planting the region's first Pinot Noir vines in a nursery in 1965. Chuck and Shirley Coury bought a farm near Forest Grove where the original owner had cultivated a vineyard of Riesling grapes in the early 1900s.

Dick and Nancy Ponzi had also just bought land. They hadn't gone to school at Davis, but Dick had fond memories of his father's winemaking, and they wanted to raise their children on a small farm. Dick's search for the right place to grow Burgundian grapes led him to buy just outside of Portland. He planted his first vines in 1970.

These four couples were working regular jobs, living as cheaply as possible, and putting all their extra time and money into their vineyards. Finding them kept us going—we were not alone. We kept getting new leads. We heard that someone had been growing grapes in southern Oregon's Umpqua Valley for years, so we drove three hours south to Roseburg and met Richard Sommer, who had started his vineyard in 1960. We tasted his wine and peppered him with questions.

That autumn, we talked about everything except why we would want to enter a field about which we knew nothing. We focused on the practicalities: What would it take to start a vineyard? Should it be in California, or would Oregon work? Here we were, two liberal-arts graduates trained in critical thinking and research, about to risk everything we owned—and we couldn't wait to jump in. I smile as I think back. Neither of us had ever farmed? No problem, we would learn. Bill had spent summers working on sheep and cattle ranches, and through high school he had a job at a nursery, doing landscaping. That sounded good enough to me. Neither of us had any business experience? We would learn. There was no tradition of fine winemaking in Oregon? We would help create one. We knew we could lose everything, but how much did we have to lose? Our professors at Stanford had told us that a liberal-arts education was training for life, that we could do anything with it. We were about to put that notion to the test.

As the bigleaf maples in the Willamette Valley turned golden, we moved beyond whether to where. Did we want to go to California, where there was an established wine-grape industry, or did we want to stay in Oregon, where there was none? California would be more expensive, Oregon more risky. By the time the leaves blanketed the ground, we had decided to stay in Oregon and focus on the cool-weather grapes that made the wines we liked best—Pinot Noir, Chardonnay, and Riesling. It was the kind of decision most easily made by people in their twenties, an age when optimism has not yet been tempered by experience.

We wanted to be part of this great experiment—creating an Oregon wine industry. The biggest lure was the challenge of growing Pinot Noir, the red grape from Burgundy that had a reputation for being difficult and had never done well in the New World. If questioned, we would have said that after producing excellent wine grapes, we would go on to make world-class wine, but our initial focus was the vineyard. We embraced the challenge before us, knowing that if we succeeded, it would be on the strength of our brains and our brawn.

From the beginning, the vineyard was Bill's baby. I mirrored his excitement and didn't want to disappoint him, but it was years before I fully experienced the passion that he felt from the start. I wanted to be a good wife and partner, and I didn't flinch at the challenge, the time commitment, or the money we put into the project. But it took time for me to feel that it was a genuine partnership. In the end, my commitment surpassed his.

After looking at possible vineyard sites all through the hills of the northern Willamette Valley, we finally found what seemed the perfect piece of land in the Dundee Hills, about thirty miles southwest of Portland. The area, known for its giant, sweet Brooks prunes, is a series of gentle hills ranging from three hundred to a thousand feet in elevation. Our eighteen-acre piece, at the five-hundred-foot level, had been an orchard, abandoned after the famous Columbus Day storm. The old prune trees sprawled across the land haphazardly, few still upright. Local lore was full of stories of the damage and death caused by that near-hurricane, which we assumed had happened recently because it was such a common point of reference for local farmers. We were shocked to learn that it had occurred in October 1962, almost a decade earlier. The stories were simply evidence of the long-term impact of weather on a farming community. They did not deter us. Perhaps because we hadn't lived through its ferocity, the storm seemed a remote, one-time event.

The old orchard had been waiting for us, the downed trees obscured by a labyrinth of blackberry vines and vetch that had blanketed the hillside over the years. Knowing that fruit trees had flourished there cinched our decision to buy the land. It meant the hillsides were frost-free in early spring when those trees had blossomed and thus would be safe for grapes, which leafed out at the same time. We bought the land for eight hundred dollars an acre and hired a local farmer to clear it. It had been just five months since the subject of a vineyard had first come up.

Yet living in southwestern Portland, so far from our property, became increasingly inconvenient. With Bill teaching at Portland State, we had only weekends to work the land. We found a farmhouse for rent about a mile from our property, and our family—Bill and me, baby Nik, and our cats, Cadwallader (Caddie) and Tigger—moved there in May 1971.

The house had a long, narrow front yard where we intended to plant grape cuttings a few inches apart in nursery rows. They would grow into small, bushy plants that could be planted as dormant rootings the following spring. We needed to get the cuttings from California, so when Bill visited his folks in the Bay Area, he and his dad went to Livermore, hoping to buy some of Karl Wente's certified virus-free Chardonnay cuttings. Bill was thrilled when Karl himself greeted them warmly in his small office. "Gonna grow grapes in Oregon, eh?" he said. "Great idea. I always wondered why no one was trying the cool-climate grapes farther north. I think you have a chance to make some great wines up there." Karl's words of encouragement endeared him to Bill forever. Bill and his dad returned home with cuttings of all the varieties we thought might grow in our cool climate—Pinot Noir, Chardonnay, Pinot Blanc, Riesling, and Müller-Thurgau (a cousin of Riesling).

Our big white farmhouse sat beside the old state highway, a picture-book place with its tall, shady trees along the front and old, untended cherry and prune orchards along the sides and back. But any romantic notions we had about country living were quickly lost. From across the narrow road, one of the area's major turkey farms assaulted every one of our senses from the day we moved in. Hundreds of white turkeys lined up at the fence to clamor at us, red jowls bobbing and beady eyes staring. From time to time huge trucks went by carrying stacks of large cages crowded with turkeys. White feathers kept floating to the ground long after they had passed. The odor of turkey manure, from merely pungent to overpowering depending on the heat and the wind direction, was the sensory backdrop for all our activities. The gentle breeze that cooled me while I worked in the vegetable garden also enveloped me in the rank smell of turkey. My nose wrinkles just thinking about it.

The house, like a number of others in the valley, was apparently the work of some barn builders who came through in the early 1900s. They built houses the way they constructed barns—framing studs set more than two feet apart, little attention to detail, no insulation. My homemade cotton curtains fluttered in the wind even with the windows closed, and the smell of turkey manure leaked in through the cracks. Over the years, residents had added sections to the original house, so that by the time we moved in, it included what had once been an animal barn in the back. Bill and I had often talked about what fun it would be to buy an old farmhouse and fix it up. Realizing what it would take to make our rented farmhouse comfortable ended that fantasy.

The cats roamed freely through the abandoned orchards, sleeping by day, hunting by night, and wreaking havoc on the mouse and gopher population. After Tigger was run over one gruesome night, Caddie did the work of two. She was a fearsome hunter and ate most of her prey outside, leaving the front teeth, whiskers, and large intestine on the doormat for us to admire. One night she came flying through the open window at the head of our bed with a large gopher clutched in her teeth. I opened my eyes in time to see Caddie and the gopher pass over my head, inches from my face. I listened to her chewing her prize for a few minutes, and then turned over and went back to sleep, making a mental note to watch where I stepped in the morning.

For the first few months, until the cats pared down the population, the mice were the most active inhabitants of our house. I learned to put my feet in my slippers slowly lest I find a living fur ball cowering in the toe. When my mother visited from Wisconsin, I sat with her at the kitchen table trying to keep her engaged in conversation so she wouldn't see the mice scampering across the floor. She saw them, of course, as soon as I stopped talking to take a breath. They only reinforced her belief that Bill and I were living in the wilderness. She must have enjoyed herself anyway (or else felt I really needed help), because within ten years she and my father had moved to McMinnville, seven miles from us, where they spent the rest of their lives.

Our house stayed warm because we kept the huge brick fireplace in the living room going fall, winter, and spring. We had plenty of firewood from downed trees, and fans in the fireplace sent waves of heat through large vents to warm the rest of the house. We splurged on new carpet for the living room, a gold shag found at a discount warehouse. Shag was in fashion, and we bought a special rake to lay all the long carpet threads in the same direction. But even with the carpet perfectly combed, the place never made it past tolerable. We were near our vineyard and the rent was only a hundred dollars a month, so we decided we could put up with it.

I had grown up on the east side of Milwaukee, among the substantial homes with large front lawns and big trees that line Lake Michigan. My gardening experience had consisted of growing a sweet potato propped on toothpicks in a glass of water, a grade-school science project. In Oregon, surrounded by fruit trees and plenty of land, I felt compelled to have a vegetable garden. Once I began, I couldn't stop. I went wild with the Burpee seed catalog, inspired by page after page of mouthwatering photos of perfect vegetables. I was sure the seeds I planted would grow into that picture-perfect produce if only I could follow the instructions on the seed packets. But did "plant in full sun" mean I should plant the seeds only on a sunny day, or merely in a sunny spot? One gardening book advised, "Harvest during the full moon." Should I be picking my vegetables at night, under moonlight, or could I pick them in daylight if there was to be a full moon that night?

That first spring, after savoring the catalog descriptions all winter, I planted everything that looked interesting, from peas to pumpkins. I kept the growing season going right into fall, but I was way out of my league. I was overwhelmed by the successes—I'd never seen so many zucchini—but I was also befuddled by pest problems. I had no idea whether the cute little bugs I saw crawling around the plants were going to help me or destroy the garden. I knew ladybugs were good, but how about the ones that had black spots but were yellow instead of orange? Captivated by the wonder of working with the earth, I came back every year with a little more knowledge and renewed hope.

While our cuttings in the front yard sprouted leaves and roots, we searched for vineyard equipment we could afford, which meant second-hand. The weekly agricultural paper, *The Capital Press,* listed the farm auctions and used equipment for sale everywhere in the valley. We needed a tractor most, but we also needed a plow and a disk to pull behind it for working the land. Bill and I, with Nik in the backpack, attended farm auctions almost every weekend. Finally we found the right tractor at the right price, an early-1960s-vintage Massey Ferguson orchard model. The auction was at the other end of the valley, so Bill had to drive our new pur-chase home, bumping slowly along country roads for forty miles. Nik and I rattled along behind in Truckeroonie, our '53 green Chevy pickup.

Truckeroonie had been Bill's first vehicle, bought while we were at Stanford. Despite a two-year rest while we were in Chapel Hill, it was feeling its age. Bill commuted to Portland in the VW camper, so when Truckeroonie broke down, I was likely to be at the wheel. I never went out in it without rain gear, rubber boots for walking in the mud, and a backpack for Nik. Hank Paul, the mechanic in Dayton, the nearest town, became my friend. Whenever I walked into his shop, his scruffy little white dog, with shaggy hair over its eyes, scampered out to greet me. The three of us would climb into Hank's big pickup and drive back to wherever Truckeroonie had stalled.

Truckeroonie—with its old green cab, worn leather seat, and long, wobbly stick shift—was full of memories. It had taken us camping in the California redwood country, where we had slept under the towering trees, and to the San Francisco Opera House, where we had watched Rudolf Nureyev make jaw-dropping leaps across the stage. Truckeroonie was our transportation whether I wore dirty jeans and hiking boots or a slinky black dress and high heels. After Bill came home one day with a shiny new sky-blue pickup, we sold the old truck to a farm kid excited to get his first wheels. I had a lump in my throat watching it drive off.

Another challenge, while we were searching for affordable equipment, was finding a way to make trellising for the vines. When we heard that the local pole-bean farmers were switching to bush beans, we jumped at the chance to buy their used poles and wire. We sorted through piles of old bean stakes to find the strongest, straightest ones, and then Bill soaked them in foul-smelling, poisonous pentachlorophenol so they wouldn't rot when he put them into the ground.

Not all our hot deals worked out. Right after Nik was born, Bill bought an old Cat 22, a Caterpillar tractor. The farmer guaranteed that it was almost ready to go, and that the cans of parts sitting around it would go together quickly. For the next two months, Bill spent all his spare time in that farmer's field, forty miles from us, fighting to put the thing together. Nik and I tried going with him, but it was boring to sit in the field and watch him try to match the pieces. He didn't give up; he finally loaded the little crawler tractor on a trailer, along with all the cans of parts, and brought it to the vineyard. He got it together, but it would turn only to the right. It was a long time before he was able to chuckle at that great money-saving scheme.

When the land had been cleared, we prepared for planting: disk, till, measure off rows, and mark the spot for each plant with a small stake. With the other early growers, we spent hours discussing the merits of various vine spacings, and row spacings, and trellis systems. We knew that the vines in the vineyards in Burgundy were very tightly spaced; both the plants and the rows were just one meter (approximately three feet) apart. But in California, typical spacing was twelve feet between the rows and eight feet between the vines. All of the equipment available in the United States was sized for California vineyards; nothing existed to farm the French spacing. We decided to use the tightest spacing we could with the equipment we had, so most of us planted our first vines in rows ten feet apart, with six feet between the vines. We all looked at practices in France and California and tried to take the best of each, after lengthy discussions of the pros and cons. We were growing the same grapes, but Oregon's growing conditions were different, and we knew we had to find our own way.

Bill orchestrated our first planting in the spring of 1972, and his family came to help. When we were ready to put the plants in the ground, I drove the tractor, with Nik in the backpack, freeing Bill to carry the heavy bundles of dormant plants and pails of fertilizer. My job was to drive down the row, stop at the right spot, and drill a hole. The hydraulic auger was mounted on the back of the tractor, so lining it up with the marker stake required prolonged twisting and looking behind me. Nik had a great view of all the activity, but at seventeen months he was not happy being cooped up, and his weight in the backpack made my job even more tiring. My back ached after the first hour.

I was rescued by Bill's parents, Betty and John Blosser, who took their vacation time to drive up from Oakland and work in the vineyard for a week. Bill's dad, an orthopedic surgeon, smiled broadly as he took my place and, driving the tractor, looked the happiest I ever saw him. I never heard him complain about the twisting, or about back pain. Grandma Betty freed Nik from the backpack, played countless games of patty-cake and "ride a cockhorse to Banbury Cross," fed him, and made sure he napped. I gratefully accepted her help. From then on, until they finally just moved to Portland, John and Betty came up every year, and we intentionally postponed some major project until they arrived.

We planted five acres that first year—one White Riesling, one Müller-Thurgau, one Chardonnay, and two Pinot Noir. When it was all over, we walked to the top of the hill and surveyed our new vineyard. I stood next to Bill, who had Nik on his shoulders, and looked out over the valley. Little sticks poked out of the reddish dirt in neat rows, and the freshly turned soil smelled clean and sweet. I was sweaty and hot, but a chill went up my spine. We had done it. We had literally put down roots.

People in the farming community around us were generally friendly and helpful, although none of the farmers had experience with wine grapes. We enjoyed Carrie and Les McDougall, the retired couple who lived in a pink ranch-style house on the large lot adjoining the top corner of our property, where we had planted our first vines. They were old and arthritic and couldn't get around well, but they kept up with the community from their lookout on the hill. Every summer evening they sat in the driveway in front of their house on folding lawn chairs, and we often joined them when we finished work. As the light faded to dusk, the four of us talked about farming and looked out across our rows of grapevines, past a few big maple trees, and down onto the patchwork of farms on the valley floor. The palette was shades of green, bathed in the last rays of the sun. The distance made it seem peaceful, but we knew that farmers worked long days, and the valley was full of activity. The McDougalls knew what was happening on every parcel of land.

"Well, golly, look at that," Carrie would say, as a tiny tractor moved slowly across the light green field on the far left. "I guess George is letting little Sam drive the tractor now." Somehow, she could tell that the tractor driver was her nephew.

Then Les would pipe up with "Look, over there," and nod toward a spray of water moving back and forth across a faraway patch of dark green. "Phil's irrigatin' his beans again tonight. Must have a good contract this year with the cannery." Then they'd point out a crew moving the irrigation in a field of broccoli and talk about how a young man had been killed when the long piece of irrigation pipe he was moving crossed an electric line.

When Les McDougall died, Bill was asked to be a pallbearer at the funeral. More than anything before it, that gesture made us feel part of the farming community.

We became closest to Ted and Verni Wirfs. We bought several parcels of their land as they slowly retired from farming. Ted and his brother, Roy, farmed together on adjoining properties on both sides of Highway 99 W, the main state highway down the valley. Roy ran Wirfs Fruit Stand for many years, selling the produce they raised. The brothers built identical houses on opposite sides of the highway. Roy had stopped farming and had sold the fruit stand and his acreage years before we arrived, but Ted and Verni continued farming well into the 1980s. After they retired, Ted liked to drive the tractor for us during grape harvest, hauling totes full of grapes from the vineyard down to the winery. His skill with the tractor was invaluable when it rained and the wet, slippery hillsides made maneuvering treacherous for less experienced drivers.

Ted had an endless repertoire of stories about his years of farming, and he and Verni were a source of comfort and encouragement. I loved to visit them, just to sit and talk. Afterward, the problems we were struggling with always seemed more manageable. We learned from them that farmers—who depended on the weather, which was fickle, and were always on the watch for pests that might destroy their crops—survived by adopting a philosophical attitude. Ted and Verni lived from harvest to harvest with a curious combination of fatalism and optimism, making the best of whatever hand Mother Nature dealt and then welcoming each new year as a fresh start and another chance. We learned not to let bad harvests and difficult times defeat us. As novices, we were grateful not only for their advice, but because they took us seriously. Most local farmers stopped short, looked at us sideways, and narrowed their eyes when we told them what we were doing. "You're growing what? Why're you doing that? Nobody's done that around here." Ted and Verni won our hearts and our loyalty by supporting us with their farming knowledge and their friendship.

Howard (Putt) Putnam and his wife, Jeannie, ran Putt's Market in Dayton, an old-time general store with wavy wooden flooring. I went to a large grocery in McMinnville to do major shopping, but Putt's was a handy stop for small items and often carried local fruit in season. Putt was chief of the volunteer fire department, and Putt's Market was the heart of the community—you could buy groceries, pay your electric bill, get a field-burning permit, find farm labor, and hear the latest local news. In-town deliveries were made on a bike with a large basket. Poker-faced and kind

Usually when I visited Ted and Verni Wirfs we were all in work clothes. For this photo, taken on their front porch, we look clean and presentable. (Photo by Tom Ballard.)

under his gruff veneer, Putt always asked about our vineyard venture. Whenever I saw him, he wanted to know when we were going to start making wine. "How's that Sneaky Pete coming along?" he'd ask.

In 1973, Bill and I decided it was time to move out of our drafty rented farmhouse. We had lived all seven years of our married life in rented housing, never more than two years in the same place. I was pregnant with our second child, and we wanted a home of our own. Our first choice was to buy a house nearby, but there weren't many and none was for sale, so we reluctantly decided to build. One of the upper corners of our vineyard property sloped west, with a stand of trees buffering it from the gravel county road. It was not a good spot for grapes, but we could site a house there, against the bigleaf maples and Douglas firs on the west side, and look east, north, and south over the vineyard from the second floor.

We went to the library for books of plans, but after scanning a few hundred we decided their uniformly boxy look was boring. When we found the books of vacation-home plans, our interest picked up. These had imaginative shapes and angles. We chose one that seemed to fit the site—an octagonal pole house. Neither of us had ever been in such a house, but we liked the idea of views from eight sides.

We hired a contractor from Sheridan, a nearby farming community, whose workers came from a local commune. We planned to have them frame the house and do the rest ourselves. Bill finished his teaching contract at Portland State and took six months off to work on the house. He did all the wiring, and we cheered when he flipped the switch and it actually worked. To save money when he put up the drywall, he carefully cut and fitted small pieces into the odd angles that an eight-sided house created. It took so much time that we decided to hire professionals to tape and ready it for painting. Those professionals complained nonstop about all the tiny odd-shaped pieces they had to tape. Then I spent a considerable amount of time painting the walls, propping myself against the ladder with my increasingly pregnant belly. We moved into our almost finished home just in time to celebrate Christmas. One month later, Alex was born.

We were thrilled finally to be in a home of our own. However, it didn't take long to discover that, while an octagonal house looks good on paper, it is full of peculiar angles that made rational furniture arrangement almost impossible. None of the rooms had the square corners required to accommodate a cupboard, a TV, or a chair comfortably. Our main living area—living room, kitchen, dining area, master bedroom, and large deck—was all on the second floor, overlooking the vineyard. The kids' bedrooms were on the first floor. Below that, a daylight basement opened to the carport. We framed in space for a motorized dumbwaiter so I wouldn't have to carry babies and groceries up two flights of stairs. But in the eighteen years we lived there, we never got around to building it. We installed a small, outward-swinging door in the basement for the cats, thinking a one-way door would keep them from bringing their wildlife catches inside. Not only did they learn to pull the door toward them and duck inside before it swung shut, they got so adept that they could open it with one paw while holding a mouse in their teeth.

We accumulated more pets, who became important members of the family. Bill, who at first firmly declared he didn't want a dog, succumbed when neighbors offered us Muffin, who reminded him of his childhood dog, Trigger. White with coarse, short hair and a curvy, upright tail, Muffin defined the term *mixed-breed*. She liked to run with our pickup through the vineyard and would position herself directly in front of the wheels so that she was, in effect, leading the way. That meant she did not have to eat the dust or exhaust fumes, and she could control our speed. I'd never seen any other dog use that strategy, and it struck me as incredibly smart. She seemed to sense where we were headed and usually guessed correctly about which way the truck was going to turn. If she guessed wrong, she went into high gear to get back into the lead position. She came to us as an adult dog and softened us up for all future pets by being sweet, smart, and loyal.

From the first, motherhood scared me. I was the youngest of four siblings, and I had never babysat or even paid much attention to children. I had no idea how to handle babies and was nervous that I would do something wrong, that I wouldn't be a "good mother." I reread my paperback copy of Dr. Spock until it was falling apart, and the only pages still intact described the behavior of older children.

When we lived in the farmhouse I was generally alone all day, sometimes in total silence except for Nik's wailing and the creaking of the rocker where I sat holding him, unable to stop the tears flowing down my cheeks. Nik just kept crying, and I felt helpless. I changed his diaper and fed him. I held him, rocked him, and sang softly to him. What could it be?

It took me a long time to loosen up enough to enjoy my baby. Later I understood that his crying reflected my insecurity, and I carry a rueful tenderness in my heart for Nik who, as the first child, shared my climb up the motherhood learning curve.

As I relaxed, I was surprised to discover how interesting, how much fun, and how individually distinctive my children were. My two boys were born three years apart: Nik, reserved and intellectual, with an unexpected silly streak; Alex, gregarious and unconventional, with an unexpected intellectual streak. They complemented each other, and the older they got, the more fun they had together. I found motherhood deeply satisfying, but never easy.

When Nik was born, I intended to be a model mother. In my world, that meant staying home with him. So I looked for things I could do from home and taught myself macramé. I made more hangings, belts, and purses than I could use and bestowed my creations on friends and family. Come to think of it, I never did see my father wear the macramé belt I made him. I sold two eight-foot hangings, one to a Portland art gallery, the other to a friend, before I decided macramé was not really what I wanted to be doing.

The truth was, I was bored. That didn't surprise me. I didn't expect Nik to satisfy my social and intellectual needs. What did surprise me was realizing that Nik was bored too. He needed to get out of the house and socialize as much as I did. After exploring the few day-care options available in McMinnville, I enrolled him in a program at the First Baptist Church. Then I got myself a part-time job writing features for the weekly *News-Register*.

I generally wrote for the "Living" section, interviewing the people the editor decided to honor as Neighbor of the Week. I didn't know why they had been chosen and usually had to pry to find out whether they were newsworthy because of their prized dahlia garden, their years of service on the local school board, or the recipe for apple pancakes a pioneer ancestor had written down and they had discovered in a trunk in the attic. I carefully typed my stories on a manual typewriter and was paid twenty-five cents per column inch. This didn't even cover Nik's day care, but since I was learning a lot about the community and having fun, I kept at it.

With the vineyard in its infancy and only a few acres planted, I had time to get involved in nonfarm activities. I joined the McMinnville chapter of the American Association of University Women (AAUW) and through my new friends learned of a teaching opportunity at Linfield, a small liberal-arts college in town. I grabbed the chance to indulge my interest in American history and do the work I had trained for. I was hired as an adjunct professor and taught for the next two years, first history of the American Revolution, and then history of women in the United States. I had my own office in the History Department and worked so hard that I managed to turn teaching one class into a full-time job. The whole experience—planning and giving lectures, talking to students, being one of the faculty—was intellectually invigorating. The department chair gave me the freedom to formulate the syllabus for the courses, and I felt as if I were in graduate school taking a tutorial, except that I was also teaching it. The material was always fresh in my mind because I was absorbing it only days ahead of my class.

*Bill and Nik enjoying the bedtime story ritual on the deck of our new house.
Nik had the important job of holding his dad's wineglass.*

Here was the stimulation I craved, and I stayed until it became a luxury I couldn't afford. I was needed in the vineyard.

Back at the vineyard full-time, I accepted Verni's invitation to join the local farmwomen's social club. The Unity Ladies Club took its name from the old Unity School District, which had ceased to exist long before many of the club members were born. Members ranged in age from forty to nearly eighty, and sometimes the older members' daughters came to meetings and brought their toddlers. We met each month at a different home where we sat around and chatted, sipping coffee or sweet punch out of flowery china teacups and eating primly off the hostess's best china. The dining room table would be covered with a lacy crocheted tablecloth and laden with platters of freshly baked cookies, homemade pies or cakes, local walnuts and hazelnuts, and dishes of candies or mints. It looked like a Norman Rockwell painting. It reminded me of the fun I had as a little girl having tea parties with my dolls and my mother, pretending I was grown up, and a lady. Here was the real thing: the ladies were very kind to me; when I was pregnant with Alex, they surprised me with the first (and only) baby shower I ever had.

Most of the women had lived their entire lives in Oregon, and our conversation focused on their interests—mainly families, health problems, and crops. Meetings always had their share of "Did you hear about . . . ?" Ruth Stoller, wife of one of the major turkey farmers, held the title of unofficial county historian, and she entertained us with tales of Dayton's past glory. In the early 1900s, stern-wheelers had brought people up the Yamhill River from Portland. That's where Ferry Street, the main street in Dayton, got its name. Ruth showed us old pictures of passengers on one of the stern-wheelers, women in long dresses and bonnets and men wearing vests and straw hats.

The club leaders were the wives of the wealthiest and most successful farmers, the ones who raised turkeys, row crops, wheat, berries, or tree fruits. No one would have guessed, then, that within twenty years all the turkey farms, and most of the orchards and berry fields, would be gone, and nurseries and vineyards would be the area's primary agricultural industries. By the turn of the twenty-first century, not a single turkey was being raised for sale in the county. The only remaining evidence of that once-proud industry was the Turkeyrama street festival, still held in McMinnville every July.

At the Unity Ladies Club in the 1970s, we weren't looking to the future. We savored the moment, gossiping, exclaiming over the hostess's culinary skills, drawing names for our "secret pals" each year, and exchanging home-made Christmas and birthday gifts. There was no reason to think our world would be any different in years to come. We could not have imagined how dramatically the landscape would change over the next two decades.

2

Winery

It was just a short walk down the gravel road to the property that belonged to David and Diana Lett, the wine-grape pioneers of the Willamette Valley. We often got together with them and the other growers to talk about our vineyards. When we had potluck dinners, everyone brought wine. There were fewer than a dozen couples, college-educated young urban professionals who had chosen to go back to the land. We didn't consider ourselves "hippies," but I'm sure each of us owned at least one tie-dyed shirt. We were all about the same age, and most of us had small children. Some of us had vineyards only; others had wineries as well. When we decided to form an organization, we immediately got sidetracked by what to call ourselves. No one liked "vineyardist" or "winemaker," because each referred to only part of the whole. Someone came up with "winegrower," which we weren't sure was a legitimate word. We discussed it at length, decided it was, and formed the Oregon Winegrowers Association.

We exchanged ideas on how to keep pesky deer from eating our young vines and other immediate practical problems. No issue was too small for discussion. We talked about what clones—plants propagated asexually to reproduce the characteristics of the parent vine—we should be planting, and we worried about viruses being introduced through unregulated importation of planting stock. We were concerned about phylloxera, an insect that attacks the roots of grapevines, and wondered whether we should try to plant our vines on grafted rootstock to protect them from this pest. We decided to go ahead and plant self-rooted vines, and then ask the Oregon Department of Agriculture not to allow vines rooted in soil, which could harbor phylloxera, into the state.

There was not much time to develop close friendships or even just sit around and chat. Everyone was busy with new families, new vineyards, and the additional jobs that supported their ventures. Bill was teaching. David Lett sold college textbooks for a publishing house, and Dick Erath worked for Tektronix. Joe Campbell was an emergency-room physician. Dick Ponzi taught at Portland Community College. Dave Adelsheim was a wine steward in a Portland restaurant. Vic Kreimeyer worked for the U.S. Forest Service, Gary Fuqua for the Bonneville Power Administration, and Don Byard for the Oregon Department of Transportation. We may have all fit the same demographic, but we probably would never have met if our vineyard interests hadn't brought us together.

Bill and I were on a steep learning curve. From the time we cleared our first piece of land in 1971 until we built the winery in 1977, everything we did—having babies, house building, farming, starting the winery—was a new experience. As soon as we put the vines into the ground, we were on an express train, with nature propelling us forward. If we didn't deal with the weeds when they were small, they quickly took over, making their removal twice as difficult. More than once our young vines were overrun by vetch, entwined in the purple-flowered plants seemingly overnight. Life was so full, and moving so fast, that we didn't have time to reflect on the wisdom of our undertaking. We fell into bed and slept soundly every night, waking only when a baby cried.

My father, Gustave Sokol, who owned a tannery in Milwaukee, Wisconsin, became our partner in 1974. He invested as soon as he was convinced we were serious about our project. His annual business trips to the

Paris leather show, "La Semaine de Cuir," had made him a wine lover, and I had acquired my own taste for wine by drinking *premier cru* (literally, "first-growth") and *grand cru* wines (Bordeaux and Burgundy's top-ranked bottlings) from his cellar. He invested only a bit of cash, but he encouraged us to expand by guaranteeing loans for us at the Milwaukee bank that handled his business. His help was crucial, because local banks thought we were just as crazy as everyone else did and were hardly eager to lend money to winery projects. With Dad's help, we were able to buy adjoining parcels of land as they came up for sale. We benefited from having our vineyards contiguous. On the other hand, financing our operation so completely through debt left us undercapitalized and financially vulnerable, a condition that plagued us for years.

Within a few years, we were farming thirty acres, almost double what we had started with and more than most vineyards at the time. Much of the new acreage came with income-producing orchards, forcing us to become orchardists while we were still struggling to learn how to grow grapes. We farmed cherries, peaches, prunes, and walnuts, and they all provided extra income while we waited for the vineyards to come into production. At that time, it took at least four years. Although the orchards distracted us from our main vineyard focus, we kept them going until, one by one, we took them out and replanted with grapes. We continued to buy neighboring land parcels until, by 1980, we owned eighty acres.

None of our property was fenced, and the deer that lived in the hills became a problem. They loved tender young grape leaves and would come into the vineyard at night and strip the plants. This was serious. Dick Erath had recommended we buy bags of some smelly stuff, rumored to be the scent of cougar balls, from the local farm store, guaranteed to keep the deer out, and we hung them at the ends of rows. When that didn't work, we went to the county and got a permit to shoot deer out of season. The permit required that the deer be gutted and brought to the county jail to feed the inmates. Bill had hunted with his father and was a skilled marksman, so one night he went out into the vineyard and shot a deer. He had no idea how to gut it. His father, the surgeon, had always done that. He came back to the house, and I got out the northern Canadian cookbook I had bought to get a recipe for wild huckleberry pie. I remembered that it had a chapter on wild game because I had been so intrigued by seeing a recipe for Jellied Moose Nose. I always wondered whether anyone actually made that. I opened the book and, with a sigh of relief, found the step-by-step instructions for gutting a deer.

There was no moon that night. We took a couple of flashlights, my cookbook, and the largest, sharpest knife we could find, and we made our way through the vineyard rows to where the deer was lying. We propped one flashlight so that it shone on the deer, and I pointed the other one at the cookbook. I tried not to look at the deer, with its big eyes locked forever in a glassy stare. "Okay," Bill said. "Start reading." He wielded the knife, squeamish but determined. We finally got the deer carcass into the pickup. Before he went off to the county jail with it, we went back to the house and changed clothes so we wouldn't get ticks or poison oak. The whole experience was so traumatic that from then on, we avoided deer hunting unless John Blosser was visiting. After a few years, the vines grew big enough that the deer were no longer such a problem.

⁘

After finishing his teaching contract, Bill had taken a job with an engineering firm. He commuted to Portland every day, leaving at six-thirty in the morning and returning twelve hours later. I was caring for the children and working part-time, first at the newspaper and later at Linfield. That left us evenings and weekends to work in the vineyard—weeding, watering new plants, training vines. We hired high-school kids who lived nearby to do hoeing and other handwork. They were eager to earn money, but we had to redo much of their work. At least one baby was conceived while that crew was working in the vineyard. We kept looking for the right people and finally had the good fortune to find two brothers, Vince and Wayne Cook, who attended Newberg High School. They showed up on time, worked hard, were skilled with equipment, and were just all-around good kids. They brought in their friends when we needed a crew to plant, weed, or pick up the rocks that kept bubbling up among the rows. Vince went on to other jobs, but when Wayne finished high school he came to work with us full-time and stayed fifteen years. We could almost set the clock by the sound of his Honda motorcycle pulling up to the house at seven-thirty every morning.

The grapevines we had planted in the vineyard in the spring of 1972 produced a small crop in 1976. We sold the grapes from our first harvest to Dick Erath and David Lett. With more acres coming on, it was time to think about the next step—a winery. We had spent everything we had on the vineyard, so financing a winery seemed overwhelming. It would be months, or even years, before the wine we made would generate enough income to recoup the up-front costs of the equipment. Pinot Noir needed to age in French oak barrels for a year and then in bottles for another six months, mandating a two-year lag between the harvest and the time the wine appeared on the market. Under the best conditions, it would take another year to sell through. White wines like Riesling or Müller-Thurgau could be on the market in six to nine months, but they wouldn't produce enough income to cover the cost of holding the Pinot Noir.

Bill and I, barely able to keep the vineyards and orchards under control, were dismayed by what a winery would entail. My father, whose new vision was a family winery, spurred us on. Bill started researching startup costs and building materials and hired a marketing consultant to help estimate income and costs for the first ten years. He hired a winery design consultant to help lay out the winery and select equipment. My father's enthusiasm grew, and he talked my three older brothers into investing.

The next step, getting permission to site a winery on our property, turned out to be an unexpectedly huge hurdle. Because of his training, Bill was a firm believer in land-use planning and didn't mind having to go to the county planning commission for approval. Oregon had just buttressed its land-use laws, the legacy of Tom McCall, one of the state's most colorful and well-loved governors. McCall took a forceful stand on controlling growth. In a CBS interview in 1971, he quipped, "Come visit us again and again. This is a state of excitement. But for heaven's sake, don't come here to live." The reaction to his off-the-cuff remark was intense and immediate, and it divided Oregonians into two groups: those who found McCall and his flamboyant style endearing and considered this just one more of his exaggerated, showstopping comments, and those who opposed McCall (mainly fellow Republicans), who saw no humor in the situation and considered his comments "inhospitable" and bad for business. The incident became part of Oregon folk history.

Governor McCall is worth a short digression because he presided over three remarkable pieces of legislation. The Bottle Bill, the first in the United States, passed in two phases in 1969 and 1971. It required deposits on beer and soda-pop bottles and cans and outlawed nonreturnable containers. The landmark Beach Bill prevented private beach development and conserved Oregon's beaches for public use. The Land Use Bill, Senate Bill 100, passed by the legislature in 1973, was the one that would directly affect the wine industry. It mandated that each county decide how the land within its boundaries should be used—what should be designated agricultural, residential, commercial, or industrial.

Bill put his planning expertise to use by getting involved in the land-use planning process in Yamhill County. One of his priorities was to convince the county planners to designate hillside land as agricultural, thereby preserving it for future vineyards. The traditional view was that the valley floor, with its deeper and richer soil, should be agricultural and the hillsides, valuable as view property, should be residential. But early winegrowers had located in the hills. Hillside soils, with their lower fertility and excellent drainage, suited wine grapes, and the hillsides gave the vines natural frost protection because they were a few degrees warmer than the valley floor. David Lett, who was also a strong land-use proponent, supported Bill. They and the other growers argued that vineyards were the wave of the future and the hillsides should be designated agricultural. The winegrowers prevailed, since there was, as yet, little pressure for residential development. Later, as Yamhill County became a bedroom community for metropolitan Portland, the designation of hillsides as agricultural, with twenty- and forty-acre minimums, was vital protection for the wine industry. Because of the efforts of those early winegrowers, the hillsides in Yamhill County are dotted with vineyards instead of trailer parks or subdivisions. In neighboring counties, where the growers were less active in shaping the law, hillside housing developments encroached on farms and vineyards as the population of metropolitan Portland expanded.

Oregon entered the twenty-first century as the only state in the nation with a comprehensive land-use program. Senate Bill 100 passed at an extraordinary time in Oregon's history, when visionary and strategic politicians from both political parties found a way to work together, thinking of future generations and the betterment of the state. With uncanny synchronicity, its implementation coincided with the development of Oregon's new wine industry.

In the same spirit, the winegrowers in our Willamette Valley association shared information and cooperated to chart a course for the new wine industry. This willingness to work together for the good of the whole was a distinguishing feature of Oregon winegrowers from the start. Despite our small number, we understood that we had the opportunity to shape the future. We thought hard about what we wanted the Oregon wine industry to look like. We met at one another's homes, since the whole industry fitted into anyone's living room. None of our homes would have qualified for a feature in *Sunset* or *House and Garden* magazine. We sat on used, unmatched furniture, in rooms decorated in a style we dubbed "Contemporary St. Vincent de Paul." First, we shared news of hot deals on equipment or supplies. Then, after passing along the address of a farmer who had stakes, wire, or used equipment for sale, we talked about what legislation we might need to protect our fledgling industry. There was never easy agreement. More than once the meetings got heated. Although I don't remember the subject, I remember one argument in which Bill became de facto spokesman for one side and Chuck Coury for another. With no resolution in sight, Chuck turned on Bill in a fury and yelled at him, "You'll rue the day you crossed me!" The rest of us stared at the two of them. We weren't sure what Chuck meant, other than that he was really, really angry. From then on, when we got hopelessly stalled in meetings, someone would smile and say, "You'll rue the day . . ." and laughter would break the tension. Not every session ended in consensus, but we kept meeting until we reached it. The group showed considerable foresight in addressing land-use issues in the early 1970s when there were few wineries, not many acres of vineyard, and seemingly endless acres of available land.

Dave Adelsheim, who started his vineyard shortly after we started ours, worked with Dick Erath and Bill Fuller to push our group toward tighter state labeling regulations. He argued that if we were going to be producing high-quality Oregon wines, we needed labeling regulations that would give them unquestioned integrity. At the time, federal wine-labeling regulations were very lax, shaped primarily by the practices of industrial producers in California and New York. A winery could legally give a wine a varietal label, such as Pinot Noir or Chardonnay, when as little as 51 percent of the wine in the bottle actually came from that variety. We didn't want wineries compromising our reputations by labeling a wine "Pinot Noir" when 49 percent of it was made with less expensive grapes. Even using cheap table grapes like Thompson Seedless would have been legal. We wanted the world to know that if the wine came from Oregon, virtually all the grapes were of the variety on the label.

Dave Adelsheim wrote up the regulations we had all agreed to and presented them to the Oregon Liquor Control Commission (OLCC), the state regulatory agency. The OLCC was not eager to be stricter than the federal law, but with the whole Oregon wine industry behind the changes, it agreed. By the late 1970s, when our new regulations went into effect, any Oregon wine with a varietal label had to contain at least 90 percent of that variety. We made an exception for Cabernet Sauvignon, requiring only 75 percent, because in the grape's French home, Bordeaux, similar varieties are often blended into the wine.

Oregon's stringent new labeling requirements influenced the federal rules, but not for another ten years. At that point federal regulations raised the requirement for varietals from 51 percent to 75 percent—better for consumers, but still far below Oregon's standard. California and Washington winegrowers accepted the federal regulations. Only the early Oregon growers pursued tighter restrictions.

As growers of Pinot Noir, the grape of Burgundy, we were outraged that some large California wineries would put a blend of cheap red grapes together and call it "Burgundy," trading on the prestige of Burgundian wines and intimating that their product would taste as if it had been made of

Pinot Noir grapes. So we devised a regulation that said Oregon wines could not be named for geographic regions unless all the grapes actually came from that place. This also precluded labeling wines Chianti, Chablis, or Champagne—all names of wine regions in Italy or France. In reaching consensus on labeling regulations and persuading the government to implement them, the Oregon winegrowers demonstrated a level of cooperation and commitment rarely found in an industry whose members are ultimately in competition.

The growers in the Willamette Valley and those in southern Oregon organized separately, each cohesive and vocal but not necessarily aligned. We knew we had to speak with one voice at the state level to lobby for changes in state regulations, but sometimes it was a challenge. The Willamette Valley growers overshadowed southern Oregon in numbers and publicity, despite southern Oregon's head start, and that imbalance, coupled with our different grapes and priorities, caused an unease that always threatened to erupt into conflict and immobilization. We went to visit them, they came to talk to us, and we simply had trouble agreeing on anything, from the best name for a statewide organization to the priorities for action. Merging required numerous organizational charter drafts. After months of negotiation and compromise, we created a fragile statewide organization in 1978 that, over the years, went through cycles of cooperation, communication breakdown, collapse, and resuscitation. The power struggle was an ongoing challenge.

As we moved ahead with our winery plans and applied for the land-use permit, we saw a side of Yamhill County that we had known was there but hadn't paid much attention to—anti-alcohol religious fundamentalism.

Without our knowledge, a few fervent winery opponents carried around petitions requesting that the county deny our permit. While the petition said nothing about God, religion, or the evils of alcohol, we found out that the leaders of the petition drive were either Mormons or members of the Church of God, a fundamentalist Christian denomination. Both groups were vigorously anti-alcohol. As long as we only farmed, we were accepted into the community. But the winery we were proposing would be something new, potentially threatening. Without warning, we suddenly found ourselves cast in the role of outsiders.

I think people didn't know what to expect from a winery in their neighborhood, and their imaginations ran wild. As the petition carriers went from house to house, neighbors got worked up, thinking about the terrible possibilities. "Do you want drunks from the winery roaming the hills?" the petition carriers would ask their neighbors. They talked about the possibility of rape. "The danger is evident. Our homes and women wouldn't be safe." Petitioners asked their neighbors to imagine the flashing neon signs that would undoubtedly be on top of the winery to attract people off the highway, a quarter-mile away. In sum, a winery would be a blight on the neighborhood, threaten the well-being of their families, and endanger their quality of life.

If I had believed all the things they said would happen, I would have been against it, too. The petition recorded fifty-three signatures. I was saddened to see the signatures of some of my Unity Club friends. No one had talked to me about their concerns—they had just signed.

Adding fuel to the religious opposition was political opposition roused by Bill's work on the county land-use plan. Saving hillsides for agriculture might have been good long-range planning, but it infuriated farmers who had wanted to divide their land into smaller parcels or build more than one house on it. After working on the county plan, Bill was appointed to the

Yamhill County Planning Commission, whose task it was to uphold the new plan. He recused himself when we applied for our winery permit. People who had been denied their petitions saw a chance for revenge. One opponent stated flatly, "Blosser kept me from getting my request; I'm sure as hell going to keep him from getting his."

The hearing, on February 17, 1977, took place in McMinnville, in the basement of the Yamhill County courthouse. The low-ceilinged hearing room was packed when we arrived. I wondered what had brought out all these people and was shocked when I found out they were there for us. Or rather, against us. We were blindsided. The fierce looks on people's faces made it clear that Bill and I were the enemy and it was their mission to defeat us. Our permit request was the second item on the agenda. The commissioners never got to the third item; our hearing took up the rest of the evening.

The antiwinery faction had turned out in force, with an attorney, people to testify, and their petition full of signatures. Many of the complaints had nothing to do with the proposed winery but spoke to vineyard issues— the use of noise to scare away birds, fear of the migrant workers employed during harvest. "Technical" reasons for opposition were that a winery would lower the water table by using too much water, cause pollution, lower property values, create traffic jams, generate offensive odor with fruit waste, promote drunkenness, be a visual blight in the neighborhood, and be incompatible with the existing development in the area. Bill quietly and methodically presented our case and painstakingly rebutted the opposing testimony, point by point. He had put in a full day of work in Portland and barely had time to grab dinner. He looked alone and vulnerable in the face of such angry opposition, and I could see him struggling to stay calm and not rise to the emotional pitch of his opponents. I was horrified by the turn the hearing had taken and scared by its intensity. I wasn't scheduled to testify;

37

I sat all alone in the sea of people, wishing I were anywhere else, and listened to people around me condemning our project. It didn't take long for my shoulders to hunch up around my ears.

A tension-relieving moment came when Howard Timmons, a retired farmer who owned a large parcel at the top of our hill, stood up to testify against the noise from our bird-scaring air cannon. He was feisty and agitated about how bothersome that was. When he finished, Bill asked him to clarify one of the allegations. Silence. The audience looked expectantly at Howard until his wife, Hazel, finally interceded to explain that he hadn't heard the question; he was almost deaf. People couldn't help laughing, even though Howard had most certainly damaged their case. The absurdity of Howard complaining about the air cannon he couldn't even hear epitomized, for us, the whole antiwinery campaign.

The planning commissioners, apparently perplexed by the strength of the opposition, questioned their staff, which had recommended approval. After making sure the opponents' arguments were unsubstantiated, they voted unanimously to approve the project and send it on to the Board of Commissioners for approval.

When we got home, Bill was exhausted and I was so upset that I finally rolled Bill's exercise bike into the living room, hopped on, and pedaled as hard as I could while breathlessly venting the anger I had controlled at the hearing. We had gone prepared to talk about land-use issues and had been confronted, instead, with a personal attack and morality questions. The people who relied on religious statements, such as "I am against the winery because of my Christian family values," were publicly calling us immoral because we wanted to have a winery. I knew that the neighbors who were most vociferously against us had done things I didn't consider very moral, and their condescension and sanctimony infuriated me. I felt persecuted. Their behavior struck me as very unchristian. This was my first encounter with prejudice boldly manifesting as the word of God, and it was a rude awakening. I'm sorry to say I have seen it many times since, especially in rural areas.

At the commissioners' hearing two weeks later, the antiwinery faction was back in force. They had another chance—to appeal to the three men who had been elected to the Yamhill County Board of Commissioners and had the final say over policy issues. Not surprisingly, the commissioners listened carefully to their electorate and did not automatically adopt the recommendations of the planning commission. Our opponents had a good shot with their appeal. This time each person who testified against us presented a picture or map showing how close they lived to the proposed winery and pointed out the dangers they faced—waste and water runoff flowing onto their property, increased traffic driving by their residences, a sinful business corrupting their family life.

We had learned our lesson at the first hearing. We were armed for battle, with neighbors and other winery and vineyard people to speak on our behalf. I had eighteen signatures on a petition requesting that any decision by the Board of Commissioners be based on facts, not fears. Most people had signed our opponents' petition simply because either a neighbor had asked them to or they were scared by the scenarios the petitioners had described. The small core of people who set out to defeat the winery proposal had stirred up a lot of commotion. By the end of my visits with the neighbors, most wanted to stay out of the fight entirely, realizing that our winery would not cause the problems they had been led to believe. By presenting a map showing the locations of neighbors who were opposed, in favor, and neutral, Bill was able to demonstrate that more homeowners in our immediate area were in favor of our application than were opposed. Bill's quiet dismantling of the opposing testimony contrasted sharply with the emotional, often illogical testimony of those against the winery.

The commissioners, probably baffled by all the turmoil over what seemed a straightforward issue, postponed their decision for two weeks. Finally, they came out in our favor. We celebrated, but the fight was not quite over. The hard core of the opposition appealed the county's decision to the courts, throwing us into a quandary. We had been waiting for resolution before starting construction. If we waited until the appeal wended its way through the courts, we would not have the winery ready for the 1977 crush. We were pretty sure the courts would uphold the county's decision, but what if they didn't? We decided to take the risk. We were rewarded with a firm decision that finally put an end to the long, emotional battle.

We had never imagined it would be such a fight. After our experience, the county made the establishment of a winery on land with a minimum number of vineyard acres an outright permitted use, on the assumption that a winery was needed to process the fruit. We blazed the trail; later wineries did not have to face the same kind of opposition.

Once the winery was built and the neighbors saw their fears were groundless, they took pride in it. Within fifteen years, the wine industry had gained sufficient status that land that had cost eight hundred dollars an acre when we started was selling for as much as fifteen thousand dollars an acre. The same people who fought us started actively promoting their properties as vineyard land. Howard Timmons's old wheat fields now produce wine grapes.

We sited the winery on a rocky knoll, unsuitable for grapes but a perfect spot to build. David Lett had bought an old turkey processing plant in McMinnville to house his winery, and Dick Erath and Chuck Coury had converted farm buildings. We joked that we would have Oregon's first state-of-the-art winery simply because we built specifically for that purpose. We chose preformed concrete panels because they were affordable, went up easily, and reduced fire danger. Excavation of the site took weeks; putting up the panels took three days. We watched as they were trucked in, set in place by a giant crane, and then welded together. After a complex system of floor drains had been installed, the concrete floor was poured. Suddenly we had a cavernous six-thousand-square-foot space waiting to be filled with winemaking equipment.

We had bought our press new and purchased the rest of the equipment used from California. We found French oak barrels that needed work and hired a cooper from California to take them apart, shave the staves down to fresh wood, retoast them over a small open fire, and put them back together. He lamented to me that coopering was a dying art and no young people were going into the barrel business. I commiserated, thinking how sad it was to lose those age-old skills. Neither of us foresaw that the art of cooperage, far from dying, would have an incredible resurgence.

We hadn't hesitated to grow grapes without any training, but when it came to winemaking, we were more cautious. We had a huge financial investment in the winery, and it was not just our money. We had a responsibility to my family, our investors, to be professional and do it right. So Bill made a trip to Napa to look for a winemaker and found Bob McRitchie, a doctor of microbiology who had been making wine at the Franciscan Winery in the Napa Valley. Bob was intrigued with the idea that wine could be made in Oregon. He and his wife, Maria, and their four children moved to McMinnville, and we became the first of the early wineries with a full-time winemaker who was not an owner.

The 1977 harvest was the first year we picked grapes for our own use—our first vintage. It started on October 10 with the yellow-hued

*Bill and I with Bob McRitchie in front of
our open-top fermenting vats. (Photo by H. Richard Johnston.)*

Müller-Thurgau, always the earliest grape to ripen. The excitement the first day we crushed our own grapes was palpable.

We hired a Mexican contractor who brought in a crew of about twenty pickers, all from the same town, and they worked as if they'd each had a shot of adrenaline. They started at seven in the morning and didn't stop to eat until they had finished. Wielding curved knives with wooden handles and leather wrist straps, they grasped the grape clusters and cut the stems with swift, short strokes. In the quiet early morning, as they started picking, there was just the sound of clusters thudding into empty buckets. As they got into a rhythm, the noise level rose. Soon the air was alive with the sounds of pickers running and shouting to each other, grapes sloshing into the totes, tractors chugging back and forth. Each picker had two plastic five-gallon pails, and each time he emptied them into the wooden tote at the end of the row the contractor gave him a ticket to turn in for pay. The pickers ran, even with full pails, shouting their numbers to the contractor, stuffing their tickets into their pants, hustling back to pick. The contractor barked instructions and warnings (in Spanish): "Don't pick so many leaves! Fill your buckets to the top! Pick the whole vine! You're leaving too many clusters on the back side!" The pickers were mostly men, but some women came. Sometimes children hung around with their parents. In their enthusiasm and haste, the pickers sometimes missed whole vines or skipped clusters that were hard to reach. I walked up and down the rows picking the fruit they had overlooked.

We tried to sort the grapes as they went into the totes, taking out the leaves and any clusters that looked underripe or diseased. I stood at the totes with the contractor to monitor the picking. Ted Wirfs brought his tractor to help our vineyard man, Wayne, lay out the totes in the morning, and then bring them to the winery as they were filled. As the totes came in, Bill and Bob weighed them and then used a forklift to dump the clusters into a large hopper on top of the crusher-stemmer before they went to the press.

Nik and Alex, then six and three, were in on the excitement; I had hired a babysitter to be with them so they could be part of our first vintage. Clad in rubber boots, blue jean jackets, and baseball caps, they watched big-eyed. Everything hummed along until the dumping mechanism on the forklift broke down. Bill and Bob knew right then that they were stuck with a lot of heavy lifting. They spent the rest of the day dumping grapes into the crusher-stemmer by hand. Fortunately, the forklift repairman came the next day.

One by one, over the course of a month, the other grapes became ready for picking. The dark purple, small-clustered Pinot Noir grapes went directly from the crusher-stemmer into large, open-topped wooden vats to ferment. Three times a day, Bob and Bill took turns punching down the hard layer of skins, called the cap, that forms at the top of the vats during fermentation. Standing on a wooden plank laid across the top of the fermenter, they punched the cap with an inverted dog dish attached to a long piece of PVC pipe. They called it their upper-body workout. About a week later, when fermentation was complete, they pumped the Pinot Noir into the press and pressed the juice off the skins. Then the young wine went into the small French oak barrels for aging.

We finished harvesting our Chardonnay and Riesling, the last of our "estate" grapes—grown in our own vineyards—on October 22. By then the days were getting colder and the fall rains threatened to settle in for the duration. Our forecasts put our first vintage at forty-five tons of grapes, for a total of three thousand cases of wine, but less than half came from our vineyards, as we had only five acres of our own in production. We bought Riesling, Gewürztraminer, and a few other varieties from a large vineyard in Pasco, Washington, called Sagemoor Farms, which belonged to friends of ours. Totes of their grapes arrived at our winery in large trucks the morning after they were picked. The Sagemoor grapes augmented our production through the early years, until local grapes became more readily available.

∴

We had a hard time deciding on a name for the winery. I imagined there was a perfect name that would call out to customers in wine shops and make them want to grab our bottles off the shelf. We just had to will that name into our consciousness. We thought of names that had Dundee in them, names that highlighted the hillsides, the vines, the river, the creeks. Nothing seemed just right. I lamented that we were simply not creative enough to come up with a magical name. The marketing consultant Bill had hired consoled us. This winery was our baby, he said. Giving it our family names would let potential customers know that real people were involved. "Remember that slogan for lacy women's bras?" he said. " 'Behind every Olga, there's an Olga'? Put your names on the line. Both your names, since you're equal partners."

So Sokol Blosser it was. After all, we reasoned, Orville Redenbacher, the popcorn king, and Smucker's, the jam people, had used their odd family names. That didn't keep them from being successful. We could do it too. Bill's friends teased him about putting my name first, but we had thought it through. We meant to use the initials of the winery as part of our logo, and Blosser Sokol would not have worked.

Once we had our name, we engaged Clyde Van Cleve, a Portland graphic artist whose work we liked, to design a wine label for us. More decision-making agony and wringing of hands ensued, but Clyde came up with a design we used, with only color modifications, for the next twenty years.

Our original label and first vintage of Pinot Noir.

The label was about three inches by three inches, with a rounded top that arched over the SB logo. The black and brown lettering on textured beige paper later seemed drab, but at the time we thought it fresh and exciting.

We debated whether to build a tasting room that would be open to the public. No other winery in Oregon had one, although Dick Erath had converted his garage into a tasting area. We were located on a busy state highway and knew we had great visitor potential. Our marketing consultant, who worked with Sterling Winery in California, advised us that a tasting room would be an indispensable public-relations tool as well as a retail sales opportunity. It turned out to be one of the best pieces of advice we received from the experts we consulted in putting the winery together.

A mutual friend introduced us to John Storrs, a Portland architect noted for his imagination and his ability to design for the natural setting. John had designed several Oregon landmarks, the best known of which was Salishan Lodge, a resort on the coast that had become an instant mid-twentieth-century architectural classic. Boisterous, tall, large-framed, and charismatic, John always dominated the space he was in. "Blueprints are just a formality," he declared; he preferred to design as he built. We enjoyed him and watched as he wandered around changing things after construction had begun—an opening here, a window there. He drove the builders crazy with his unconventional style. They grew to dread his visits, as they knew he would find something he wanted redone. But the result was better for it.

In the summer of 1978, Sokol Blosser opened the first Oregon tasting room designed specifically for that purpose. The gray stucco tasting room hugged the knoll and coordinated well with the gray concrete of the winery. The existing large oak and maple trees and our landscaping with native plants provided color and contrast. On a clear day, Mount Hood loomed majestically, perfectly centered in a large east-facing window. Other windows looked out over vineyards and the valley beyond. Besides a tasting area, the space contained a small kitchen, one tiny office, and two bathrooms. The back door opened to a breezeway that connected the tasting room with the winery. There was also another door six feet off the ground, anticipating the big deck we wanted but couldn't afford. That door remained nailed shut for the next twenty years until, in the late 1990s, the deck was finally added.

*Bill and I checking the plans during the building of the tasting room, aided by
Alex (in his favorite Big Bird shirt) and Muffin, who was always wherever we were.*

Once we had the tasting room, the challenge was to get people to visit
on weekends, when we were open. Wine touring in Oregon was, as yet,
virtually unknown. The *Willamette Week,* Portland's scrappy alternative
newspaper, sent its food writer, Matt Kramer, out to interview us. He was
about our age and spent half the day with Bill and Bob and me. We found
out almost as much about him as he did about us — his transition from New
York to Portland to go to Reed College, how he had graduated from Reed
in three years, his restaurant reviewing, and his iconoclastic approach to
the world in general. We enjoyed his sharp wit. The resulting article, complete with large individual pictures of the three of us, covered the whole
front page of the *Willamette Week*'s food section of the July 17, 1978, edition. The article emphasized how carefully we had planned our venture

and how we were the first winery in Oregon to begin on such a large scale. The idea that 4,500 cases could be considered large-scale indicates just how small the Oregon wine industry was.

We wanted to let everyone know we were open for business, and we sent out mailers to friends and friends of friends. We threw a big party. Slowly the word spread. I spent weekends behind the bar welcoming people and pouring free tastes that we hoped would lead to sales. It was months before we could hire any help and years before we could be open more than weekends. The kids were always with us. During cherry season the first year, eight-year-old Nik demonstrated his entrepreneurial skills by showing up with fresh cherries from our orchard to sell to the customers. Taking his cue from the way we worked the tasting room, he offered free tastes. He never failed to sell out.

If we were going to encourage people to take weekend drives to the winery, we had to make sure they could find us easily. How were they going to know, as they drove along the highway, that they were getting close to Sokol Blosser? A sign at the entrance to the winery wasn't enough. People needed some advance warning so they could slow down to make the turn. Ever since Lady Bird Johnson's roadside cleanup campaign and the subsequent passage of the Federal Highway Beautification Act, Oregon had strictly regulated signage. We couldn't just put up a sign saying "Sokol Blosser Winery, ahead 300 ft." This was a problem for all the new wineries, most of which weren't right off a main road as we were but were hard to find on county roads.

To compensate for the fact that billboards were banned, the federal government came up with a new program to allow "tourist-oriented directional signs" (TODS) that informed but did not advertise. The signature blue-and-white TODS blossomed under the Carter administration. Large "logo" boards appeared near freeway exits to indicate the availability of gas, food, and lodging, and a pilot program was under way to allow signage for

*I hosted the tasting room, pouring wine for customers on weekends.
On the top left is a large framed vineyard needlepoint my mother
had done for us. Below that are two of our first wine awards.*

recreational or cultural destinations. The head of the U.S. Department of
Transportation during the Carter administration was an Oregonian, Neil
Goldschmidt, so the winery owners thought it would be easy for Oregon
to become part of the pilot program and get TODS signage for wineries.
To the dismay of the good Oregon winegrower Democrats who applied,
the request was denied. Ironically, it was approved when we reapplied during the Reagan administration.

   Federal approval was just the first step, since the program had to be accepted and administered at the state level. Oregon State Senator Nancy Ryles championed the wineries' cause, sponsoring the legislation to create an Oregon TODS program that would include wineries. Oregon's first blue TODS sign was installed ceremonially at Sokol Blosser by Governor Vic Atiyeh. Senator Ryles also nominated me to the board of the Travel Information Council, which oversaw these signage programs, and I served on that board for the next six years.

Helping the fledgling wineries get directional signage was one of the last of many good works by Senator Ryles. Soon afterward, she developed a brain tumor and died. It was a loss for Oregon. I greatly admired her as a successful politician who had maintained both her style and her integrity while getting things done.

Bill's leadership in acquiring TODS signage definitely helped us and the other young wineries encourage visitors. But some of Bill's ideas for promoting our tasting room were not quite as practical. It was his bright idea that we could add a little pizzazz by having peacocks roaming around the grounds. It was just our luck that, at the annual Newberg Rotary Club Pancake Breakfast, one of the silent-auction items was three peacocks— two males and a female. We didn't know anything about peacocks, but here was our chance. Bill wrote his name on the bidding sheet. He was the first bidder. We had breakfast and strolled around the park for a while, and when we went back his was still the only name. Much to our surprise, we drove home with three peacocks in the backseat. They sat quietly in three large cardboard boxes with holes cut in the back for the males' long tail plumage to hang out. We soon learned why we had been the only bidders.

We took our new pets home first, rather than to the winery. I imagined that when we let them out, they would immediately start strutting around, fanning their tails and looking beautiful. But when we opened the boxes, there was a great whoosh and all three of them disappeared into the trees.

We hadn't realized they could fly. I called a turkey-grower friend to see if she knew anything about peacocks. She didn't. Although we could hear their plaintive cries from time to time, they were out of sight. We figured that was probably the end of our peacock project. It was, almost. About a week later, one of the males reappeared. We lured him in with dry cat food. We named him Vern, for the character on the Gallo wine cooler ads we had been watching on television, because the name and the connection amused us.

Vern the peacock was truly gorgeous, and he fanned his tail feathers whenever he thought someone was looking. I caught him many times fanning his feathers in front of a shiny hubcap on a car in our driveway. Was he admiring himself, or thinking he was showing off before another male peacock? Vern took up residence on the flat top of the doghouse we had built on our deck, right outside a large living room window. He could look in and see us, and we always knew when he was there. He slept there every night, winter and summer, and wandered around outside during the day, often bounding into the trees but never straying very far. In the five years he lived with us, he never even got close to the winery.

In the early months of 1979, when Nik was eight and Alex was five, Bill and I suddenly realized that our boys were growing up fast and we missed having a baby around. Impulsively, I stopped taking birth control pills. It wasn't long before I was pregnant. The boys were excited, since they were old enough to have proprietary interest in a new brother or sister. We had planned to tell Bill's parents at a family gathering, but Alex, full of importance with his new knowledge, blurted out, "Mom's going to have a baby!" to Grandma Betty and Grandpa John as soon as we arrived, before we even got through the front door.

Because I would be thirty-five when the baby arrived, the age after which pregnancy was considered riskier, my doctor recommended that I undergo a new procedure, amniocentesis, to check the health of the fetus. I agreed to the procedure and then waited six weeks, which seemed an eternity, for the report. After reassuring me about the baby's health, the nurse who called asked if I wanted to know the baby's sex. When she told me I was going to have a girl, I burst out crying, surprising myself at my emotional reaction. I hadn't realized until then how much I had wanted a daughter.

Alison was so much younger than her brothers, I worried they would boss her around—a predicament I knew well from my own childhood with three older brothers. But Alison seemed born to take charge and quickly proved she could hold her own. One night, when Bill and I had prevailed on the boys to babysit, we returned home to find Alison clutching a large wooden spoon while playing Lego with her brothers. We knew something had happened. It turned out that after we had left, the boys had gone off to play, leaving Alison alone. She didn't like being ignored and decided she wasn't getting the babysitting to which she was entitled. So she got a wooden spoon from the kitchen and ran after them with it until they paid attention to her. They were more amused than scared, but they gave in and played with her. The episode firmly established Alison's reputation for not taking any guff and became a family joke. Many years later, when she got married, Nik gave her a wooden spoon.

We had started off 1971 with a new baby, a wild business idea, and a bare piece of land. By the end of 1979, we had three children, a mature vineyard, and a fledgling winery. What a decade it had been.

3

Dirt

My father, who loved to say that the best fertilizer is the farmer's footsteps on the land, had been urging Bill to devote his full attention to the vineyard and winery. Shortly after Alison was born, in early 1980, we decided the winery could afford to pay its president, so Bill was able to quit his job in Portland. Every morning after breakfast, he walked through the vineyard down the hill to the winery. I watched him disappear among the vines, wearing a cotton shirt, jeans, and vineyard boots but still carrying his briefcase— the only vestige of his city job. His suit and tie collection was relegated to the back of the closet, reserved for sales trips and meetings with the banker. He no longer spent two hours commuting and it felt as if he were closer, but in reality it just meant that he could spend more time working.

Having Bill at the winery on a daily basis changed the existing dynamics. I had been running the tasting room pretty much on my own, but with Bill there I was less autonomous, and I didn't want him to be my boss. I raised this point, and we looked for an arena that could be mine. Why not the vineyard? I was already keeping the books and writing the checks. I decided I could do the physical work, too. During the 1970s, after the initial plantings, I had been busy having children and, after my short stints at Linfield and the *News-Register,* working on the winery project. I had been involved with the vineyard only from the sidelines. Wayne Cook, our vineyard man, had been doing most of the work. Bill and I decided I could shift my focus to the vineyard, and I found Wayne was glad to have the help and the increased attention to his part of the business.

I worked in the vineyards every day for much of the 1980s. Wayne patiently trained me on all the equipment. Although I was his boss and twelve years his senior, he took time to show me things—little things, like where to find the grease fittings on each piece of equipment and how to refill the grease gun from the bulk grease barrel, and big things, like how to use the forklift to load totes of grapes or cherries onto our big flatbed truck, tie down the load, and drive carefully. I started with almost zero knowledge, so I was grateful that he was never arrogant or overbearing. Little by little, I moved from needing to have Wayne tell me what had to be done and get the equipment ready to making the decisions and doing the work myself. I gathered a store of information about things that I had never before even wondered about. I'd never had an urge to know how a piece of heavy equipment attached to the back of a tractor, but now I knew how to maneuver the tractor into position so I could do it without heavy lifting. I'd never imagined driving a twenty-foot flatbed truck, but now I knew how far into the intersection to go before starting to turn a corner. Not only did I learn to use the equipment, but I also learned what needed to be done in the orchards and vineyards—pruning, fertilization, spraying, canopy management, crop estimates, harvest procedures. I took a farm management class to get a better understanding of the business I had taken on.

I threw myself into my vineyard work, wishing I could inhale all the new information. I relished my new skills. Crouching to grease a piece of farm equipment, my overalls covered with dust and my hands and nails stained dark brown from the grease, I'd suddenly wonder what my high school friends would think if they could see me now. I'd remember the photo my parents proudly displayed of me as a debutante. I smiled out from the frame, elegant in my white strapless gown and elbow-length kid gloves,

I was eighteen when this photo was taken at my parents'
house, with our family dog. (Photo by B. Artin Haig.)

my hair in a French twist. It was about as far from my vineyard life as I could imagine, and it made me smile now, not only at the contrast but also at the unexpected turns my life had taken. Who would have guessed? I would not have changed places with anyone.

Something happened to me when I got out into the vineyard. It both freed my spirit and tied me to the land. Being responsible for the farm focused my attention and stimulated my intellect, but being in the orchards and among the vines penetrated right to my gut. It gave me a sense of oneness with the land and a fulfillment I had never imagined. I could have lived my whole life in a city and never discovered those feelings. Until then, I'd often participated with more fervor than I felt. After I took over the vineyards, I finally began to take emotional ownership of the project that had been swirling around me and dominating my life for a decade. My passion for our venture grew steadily from then on, until finally it surpassed Bill's.

Even now, I can close my eyes and imagine myself walking down a row of vines early on a summer morning. My feet are wet from the dew soaking through my boots. The air is fresh, cool on my skin, and very still. No breeze, so it's a good day to spray sulfur. The vines are bright green and lush with new growth. The sun, just touching the vines, will soon be intense. If I am lucky I will spot a nest, probably from one of the bright yellow goldfinches, hidden in the vine canopy.

Or it is the end of a summer day, when the sun casts long shadows and all the colors look deeper and richer. Above me the swallows swoop and swirl, picking bugs out of the air. A small breeze makes the growing tips of the vines wave gently. I can feel the heat of the day fade as the sun starts to set and a hush settles over the land.

In October, during harvest, the vineyard starts the day shrouded in mist. Viewed from the vineyard's highest point, only the tops of the tallest Douglas firs poke through, reminding me of a Japanese landscape painting. In

I had finished pounding posts for our new plantings, and as I returned to the equipment shed, little Alison ran out to greet me. This has always been one of my favorite pictures.

the foggy wetness the pickers start, breaking the dew-covered spiderwebs that stretch across the rows. By noon, the day will be gloriously sunny, with the crispness in the air that is autumn.

In winter I see the skeleton of the vineyard, the trunks and canes of the vines stark without their leafy cover. Its austerity is striking, whether cloud-shrouded and bleak with rain or snow-covered and glaringly bright. The vines sleep a long time, from December to April. By then I am eager for the vineyard to come alive. My heart sings as the swollen buds start to unfurl into tender green leaves, pink-hued around the edges. Baby clusters emerge with tendrils like tiny curls. The birds start nesting again. The air feels soft. What will this season bring? It could be a great year. A farmer's hope is always highest in the spring.

One summer morning the winery crew discovered a fluffy ball of fur outside the back door of the tasting room. They called me at the house and I came down to find a scared, shy little puppy, with honey-colored hair and a long, fluffy tail. I took her home. She was the color of a fresh whole-wheat bagel, and Bagel became her name.

Bagel enchanted us. She had the soft hair and floppy ears of a cocker spaniel, but her other features were too mixed to discern her parentage. Muffin taught Bagel her trick of running ahead of the truck. Bagel learned while she was still a puppy, and she would get running downhill so fast that her legs would get tangled up. She would end up rolling head over heels until she could stop. She learned fast, though. Not once was either dog run over by the vineyard truck.

The tractor, however, did run over Bagel once, with me at the wheel. I hadn't seen her lie down behind the tractor to lick herself, and I started to back up. She yelped, and my heart plummeted when I realized what had happened. I took her to the vet, and by some miracle, she was only bruised. What saved her was that she was lying in soft dirt, and the large tire cleats just fitted over her little body. Not only was the experience traumatic for both of us, it was profoundly embarrassing to have to explain that I had run over my own dog.

The accident took its toll, though, because within six months Bagel developed epilepsy. She must have been terrified when she had her first seizure; I'm sure she'd had them before I witnessed one. We were in the vineyard when she suddenly started convulsing. I had never seen anything like it. Feeling helpless, I just sat next to her, talked to her while she was shaking, and then picked her up and held her when it was over and she was limp and scared. The vet explained that animals develop epilepsy just like humans, and it can be controlled with medication. He put her on phenobarbital, often used as a relaxant or sleeping pill for humans.

For a short time I was taking medication too, and Bagel and I had a morning routine. I would take my little white pill and then give Bagel her little white pill at the same time, usually in a piece of cheese. One summer morning I was preoccupied, thinking about directions for the Caterpillar operator coming to clear some orchards, and I took Bagel's pill by mistake before I had a chance to stuff it into the cheese. I had already swallowed it when I realized I'd just taken a sleeping pill before going out to work in the vineyard.

I had to keep going, but I was in a fog. I moved in slow motion all morning. Finally, in midafternoon, I was able to collapse into bed. The kids hooted when I told them, loving the idea that their mom had made such a stupid mistake. The episode of Bagel's pill passed into family lore.

After the onset of epilepsy, Bagel rode more in the pickup. She bounded in whenever we opened the door for her and didn't seem to care where we were going. If the seat was occupied, she curled up on the passenger-side floor. But if we were alone I invited her up on the seat, where she sat straight and proud, staring ahead—a model passenger.

Bagel lived a long, happy life for a dog who started out as an abandoned puppy and lived her adult life with epilepsy. When we moved into Portland in 1991, we couldn't take Bagel along, but she must have had an angel watching out for her. A woman working part-time in our tasting room fell in love with her and took her home. She had other dogs, but Bagel became the queen bee and ruled happily for many years. Every year we would get a Christmas picture of Bagel with a big red bow, looking supremely happy and very regal.

⋮

Soon after I started in the vineyard, we witnessed Mother Nature's stunning demonstration of her raw power. On the morning of May 18, 1980, Mount Saint Helens erupted with a force that sent a plume of ash fifteen miles into the air and created the largest landslide in recorded history. A wall of logs and mud flowed down the Toutle River, leveling everything in its path—forests, homes, roads, bridges, wildlife—and leaving miles of desolation blanketed in gray ash.

It was a Sunday, and we had been visiting Grandma Betty and Grandpa John in Tigard, about seventy-five miles from Mount Saint Helens. We were about to leave when the eruption began. From their hilltop, we watched in silent amazement as the mountain spewed rocks and sent up a huge, roiling cloud of ash.

I had loved Mount Saint Helens for its perfectly rounded, snowy white peak. It was part of Portland's northward view, as Mount Hood was to the east. It was the site of summer cabins and a beautiful little lake, called Spirit

Lake, with a scout camp and a famous lodge. Within minutes it was changed, its graceful peak entirely gone. When the eruption stopped and the air cleared, the mountain looked like a soft-boiled egg, sitting upright in an eggcup, with its top evenly sliced off.

The possibility of an eruption had been in the news for weeks, and we had watched endless television interviews with people who had to evacuate their homes. One old man refused to leave and, of course, vanished without a trace. Still, the actual explosion surprised everyone.

Ash drifted far beyond the area desolated by the eruption. As far away as Portland, the gray dust clung to grass and shrubs for months. A thin layer of ash landed on our vineyard, but it barely covered our hillside and didn't cause any harm. We drove to Hillsboro, northwest of us, where the ash was almost an inch deep, and Nik and Alex gathered it in buckets to keep as souvenirs. Then they got the bright idea of putting it in little bags to sell to tasting room visitors. It was so successful that I never had to deal with buckets of leftover volcanic ash.

Local farmers plowed in the ash, the crops suffered no harm, and the 1980 eruption of Mount Saint Helens took its place in local lore next to the Columbus Day storm of 1962.

After we bought Ted and Verni's producing orchards, life seemed to be one harvest after another. Orchards had never been part of our business plan, but we felt we had to keep the producing orchards going until we could afford to take them out and plant grapes. Until then, we needed the small income they generated. We started with cherries in late June or early July, picked peaches July through August, and moved to prunes in late August, grapes in September and October, and walnuts in November. The bounty of fresh fruit threatened to overwhelm us. For the first few years, I felt it was my duty not to let any go to waste. Before owning orchards I had never eaten a fresh Royal Anne cherry, but canned ones had been a special dessert when I was a child. How much better they were, fresh and ripe off the tree. And I was farming ten acres of this fabulous fruit. The whole family would go down after dinner and wander from tree to tree, plucking the biggest ones and popping them into our mouths. We called it grazing in the cherry orchard.

I canned them, froze them, pickled them. I made jam, preserves, and cherry brandy. I ran out of recipes and ideas for them, and for the peaches and prunes. Finally, I realized I simply could not use, or give away, all the fruit, and some would have to go to waste. When I accepted that, life became easier.

The first orchards we removed were the peaches. Even after we had taken out all our trees, Wayne and I would go down to help Ted and Verni pick and sort their peaches for the fresh market. It was too big a job for the two of them, and they were so good to us that we were glad to help. The smallish trees were so laden with fruit that Ted had to prop up the limbs with stakes to prevent breakage. Harvest started about five in the morning, while the peaches were still cold and firm and wouldn't bruise from handling. We wore harnesses with two-gallon aluminum buckets attached so we had both hands free to pick. Unlike cherries or grapes, which could be harvested all at one time, peaches had to be picked from the same trees every few days, as they ripened. Here was one place I couldn't include the kids. Alex wanted badly to help me pick, but his hands were too small to get around the whole peach and twist it off without either bruising it or tearing the skin. Sometimes he would walk down to the peach orchard, about a quarter-mile away, to find me when he got up. One time he came running over to say he had just seen a three-foot blue jay in the vineyard on the way down. I laughed and wondered what it could have been. Turned out he had found a neighbor's extremely valuable hyacinth macaw, which had been missing.

The first peaches of the season, in late July, were Suncrest. Then came Red Haven, Hale, and finally Veteran in late August. They had different characteristics. Some were fuzzy, others smooth; the pit stuck fast to the flesh of some and fell free in others; the skin slipped easily off, or wouldn't separate; the coloration varied from hues of yellow to gold to red-orange. But ripened fully on the tree, they were all heavenly. It was not only the flavor, sweet and juicy; a fully ripe peach has a perfume, intense and captivating. No other fruit we grew enveloped the senses so completely.

Verni sorted while Ted, Wayne, and I picked. When we got too far ahead, I'd switch and help Verni sort. Sorting meant looking at each peach and putting the perfect ones carefully into one set of wooden boxes, stem side down, and the almost perfect ones into another. Those with bad spots or torn skin had to be discarded. We would put aside some of the better-looking discards for breakfast. By the time we finished picking for the day it was almost eight in the morning, and we were hungry. We rewarded ourselves with hot coffee, the ripe peaches we had stashed, and freshly baked coffee cake from Verni's oven. We sat as long as we could, until finally someone would say, "Well, guess it's time to get back to work." We stacked the flats of beautiful, perfect peaches, and the flats of not perfect but still beautiful ones, in Ted's pickup, and he and Verni took them to the fruit stand. Then Wayne and I would go back to start our day in the vineyard.

❧

Cherry season had its own rituals, from bringing in the bees in March to waiting in a long line of trucks to deliver the ripe fruit to the processor in early July. There was nothing easy about any of it, especially with the big old trees that comprised our orchard. Work began in the spring, as soon as we had a few dry days and could get in to work the soil. The first step was to hook the tractor to the big old rusty cover-crop disk that came with the property and break up the soil, going first one direction and then across it at a ninety-degree angle. The disk had big rocks wired on top to give it enough weight to cut through the thick grass that had grown over the winter. When the soil dried enough, we went through with our large rototiller. The last step was to pull a large log behind the tractor to make the surface flat and smooth. Disking and tilling were done slowly, to get the maximum effect. After that it was possible to zip around pulling a spring-tooth cultivator behind the tractor, to keep the orchard weed-free. I grew to love doing that. Putting the tractor through its paces with the spring-tooth— ducking tree limbs, and turning on a dime around the trees—I felt one with my machine the way I imagine a rider feels taking her horse through an obstacle course.

The trees bloomed in March, and we contracted with a local apiary to bring in beehives to pollinate the blossoms. We hoped for sunny days so the bees would be active. All too often it was so cold the bees wouldn't come out of their hives, and the beekeepers had to come to the orchard to feed them. The cherry orchard in full bloom was magical. Delicate white blossoms with a touch of pink covered the trees and gave them a gauzy, ethereal quality. I liked the heady feeling of standing in the middle of the orchard surrounded by the thirty-foot trees in sweet-smelling bloom. The bees produced a steady hum, buzzing from one blossom to another.

Our cherry trees were old and large, with thick trunks. Their branches hung low, making picking from the ground easier. We hired crews of Mexican workers to harvest. It was always difficult to find pickers, because strawberry harvest was at the same time and promised more money with less work. Somehow, I always managed to find a crew. They often arrived early and cooked breakfast before work. The smell of tortillas, onions, and eggs would greet us as we came down to start the picking. These men worked hard but still had time for animated conversation and jokes, and the sounds of their lively camaraderie filled the air.

There was no federal program allowing foreign farmworkers, but that didn't stop them from coming or us from hiring them. There was always an abundance of Mexican farmworkers in our area, and we were lucky to have them. It was generally known that most of the workers entered the country illegally, though they always had papers to show when asked. The black market must have been huge. The whole situation existed under the table. Everyone knew about it; nobody talked about it.

Most of these workers associated themselves with a contractor who procured work for them and supervised his workers on the farm. The farmer wrote one check for the work to the contractor, who then paid the workers. We used a contractor for all our harvesting, and I never knew how much of the check actually went to the workers. I asked how much the workers were paid per bucket of grapes, for example (fifty cents a bucket in the 1980s), but I had no way of knowing what they actually received, and I paid the contractor by the ton, not by the bucket. It was clear that the contractors did well. They drove up in large, shiny pickups with flashy accessories—lights on top of the cab, expensive wheels, special bed liners, large tool chests. In contrast, the pickers' cars looked as if they had come straight from the junkyard.

We supplied each picker with a two-gallon aluminum bucket, a harness, and a ladder. The old wooden ladders had come with the orchard and were heavy and difficult to work in among the cherry limbs. After the cherries were dumped into large wooden totes, we loaded them onto our truck and took them to the brine plant at the end of the day.

A few years after we learned the rituals of handpicking, mechanical harvesting became popular. We had to prune away the low-hanging branches so the machines could fit under the trees. Two large self-propelled machines lined up on opposite sides of a tree. One machine grabbed the trunk and shook it with great force; the other captured the cherries that fell and conveyed them to a tote. The machines moved from one tree to another, working their way down the rows much more quickly than handpickers could.

The machines had some advantages. Finding pickers had become more and more difficult, and machine harvesting was faster. However, there were disadvantages. Another grower owned the custom harvesting equipment and picked for a number of cherry growers, who usually wanted to pick at the same time. The weather made timing crucial, and we had little control over the scheduling for the machines. When the machines broke down, work stopped altogether. Part of the ritual of machine harvesting was waiting around while a mechanic tinkered with them. Moreover, there was something unnerving about watching a majestic tree ferociously shaken. I knew it could not be good for the tree.

After we'd done mechanical harvesting for about four years, the cannery decided the machines weren't getting enough fruit with stems and encouraged growers to go back to handpicking. They did this by raising the price paid for handpicked fruit to almost double that of mechanically harvested fruit. This meant we wanted our low-hanging branches back. We immediately changed our pruning, but it took years to recover that growth. Meanwhile, the pickers had to lug ladders and reach high to fill their buckets.

Rain during harvest was also a challenge. If the cherries were ripe when it rained, they would absorb the water. If the sun came out right after the rain, they would split and be rejected at the cannery. It always rained a little while the cherries were ripening, and sometimes it rained a lot. One year we tried using an empty air-blast sprayer to dry out the cherries after a rain shower. They split anyway.

Delivering the handpicked cherries was another ritual. After I got proficient with the big truck, I would make the trip with one of the kids—Alex always wanted to come—and Bagel, who was willing to go anywhere as long as she could ride. Thirty totes, three layers of ten totes each, put our truck at its maximum load. I tied it down carefully, and drove slowly to avoid sudden stops.

During the peak of harvest, there would be a string of trucks at the end of the day, waiting to be unloaded and sampled. Small pickups, straining under the weight of one tote, alternated with large flatbed trucks carrying many layers of totes. We sat in the long line, with the doors open to catch the breeze, and waited for our turn to pull up, untie, and watch the forklift unload and weigh the totes. The slow-moving line of trucks combined with the fast-wheeling forklifts, loading and unloading, looked like a choreographed dance.

Our cherry earnings depended on how well our cherries fared in the grading, and the cannery weighed and graded the cherries while we watched. The forklift brought totes over to the grader, who put handfuls from random totes into a small bucket, and then examined each cherry and put it in one of three piles. Perfect cherries with stems, the ones that could go to the drinks-cocktail market and fetched the highest price, went into pile number one. I wanted to see that pile grow. The second pile was perfect cherries without stems, suitable for the baking market and not worth as much. The third pile was rejects—cherries that were split or showed any rot. My heart sank every time a cherry went in that direction. The uncertainty of which pile each cherry would end up in gave drama and emotion to the grading process. After sorting, the grader weighed each pile, calculated its percentage of our sample, and applied that percentage to our whole load. Growers tried to "top-dress" their totes, putting the best cherries on top, but the graders knew to dig down to get the samples. During cherry harvest, the cannery stayed open to receive cherries long past dark, often until midnight.

We farmed the cherries longer than the other fruits. In 1987, with relief but also nostalgia, we took out the last cherry trees. Finally we could give our entire focus to our vineyards. But alas, there was no more grazing in the cherry orchard after dinner.

∵•

Each new vineyard year starts in the winter, when the vines are dormant, with pruning away most of the previous year's growth. A fruiting cane is left on each side of the trunk for the coming season, and short spurs are left close to the head, near the top of the vine's permanent trunk, for the following year's canes. It is done in January, February, and March, when the weather is miserable—pouring rain, cold and windy, or just gray. We wore layers of long underwear and flannel underneath yellow rain pants and slickers. Rubber boots and fingerless wool gloves completed the well-dressed pruner's look. Armed with our sharpened loppers, we marched out to address the vines. Deciding which fruiting canes to leave required skill. The rest was just cutting the growth back, repetitive and ultimately boring.

When we pruned in the 1980s, it took three passes down each row. First, we made the pruning cuts. Next, we pulled the brush off the trellis wires. This involved cutting, too, and required safety glasses because the grape tendrils cling tightly to the wire and a cane could snap in our faces. We piled the pulled canes in the middle of the row, to be chopped by a flail mower as soon as the ground was dry enough for us to drive the tractor through the vineyard. Last, we went through and secured the remaining canes to the wire with twist ties. Once the canes were tied and the prunings flailed, the vineyard was ready for spring. This job had to be finished before the buds started to puff up and leaf out, since the pruning process could easily rub off the fragile buds.

During my years in the vineyard, pruning season was one of the most sociable times, despite the fact that it took place during the worst weather of the year. In addition to our own small crew, I hired three to four extra people every winter to help. Since the late 1980s, most vineyard work has been taken over by Hispanic workers, but during the early 1980s we had a mostly Anglo crew of genial counterculture folks. For two or three consecutive years I hired two brothers from Tennessee who somehow drifted into our lives and another young man who was taking time out from teaching English to Japanese businessmen in Tokyo. Another year I hired a young accountant who wanted to learn about vineyards. But our most faithful and longest-lived worker was Ofelia, a local woman who had been born in Mexico but achieved U.S. citizenship while she worked with us. After years as migrant workers, Ofelia and her first husband had settled in Dayton, in their own home, and raised eleven children. Her husband had died, and while I knew her she lived with one of the prominent labor contractors of the area—until he ran off with a much younger woman. Ofelia had the beauty and fire of a flamenco dancer, and one would never guess how hard she had worked all her life. Before coming to work at the vineyard every morning, she got up early to take care of her chickens and make fresh tortillas for her family, often bringing some for us for lunch. She worked in the vineyard all day, doing the same jobs as the men, and then went home to help her grown children or take care of her grandchildren. I never heard her complain.

On rainy days, we would prune with our hoods up and our heads down, each in our own row, addressing the vines, with only the sound of the loppers breaking the silence. But when the rain stopped, we would throw back our hoods and the conversation would start:

Terry: "What'd you guys do last night?"

John: "We thought we'd check out the Dumpsters behind Safeway."

Ben: "You should see the stuff they throw away. We found a gazillion boxes of cookies that had never been opened and packages of macaroni and cheese. What a haul!"

Wayne: "They probably had to throw them out. Past the expiration date."

Ben: "They're still good, though."

Susan: "Let me get this right. You went exploring Safeway's garbage last night?"

John: "Yeah. We discovered we could do half our grocery shopping that way. You can shop inside the store if you want; we'll go Dumpster diving."

The conversation veered off here to a comparison of the Dumpsters outside the various McMinnville grocery stores, then Tony's anecdotes about teaching English in Japan, and finally a critique of the latest hit singer, Cyndi Lauper. At that point, Terry stopped the conversation by belting out "Don't Go Breakin' My Heart," à la Elton John and Kiki Dee, and we sang until it was time for lunch.

At noon we would sit in the vineyard office—the basement of our house—while we dried off and warmed up, the ambrosia of wet rain gear, tuna sandwiches, corn chips, and fresh oranges permeating our conversation. Someone had given me a book called *Totally Tasteless Jokes,* and we took turns reading it. The jokes were pathetic and we mostly moaned at them, but then one would strike us as hilariously funny, and the laughter felt good. Occasionally—just often enough to keep us from rain-induced depression—the sun came out and the whole world looked different: blue sky, bright sunshine, and snow-covered Mount Hood looming over the vineyard, its majestic peak alternately tinged with pink, gold, or blue. What a glorious feeling to be working outside! How lucky we were to be working in the vineyard! We strode up the rows more boldly and sang louder on those days.

⋮

The crucial first step in managing the vine canopy, to prevent disease and promote quality fruit, is trellising. If we didn't trellis grapevines, they would sprawl all over the ground. There are many ways to do it; the number of different trellis systems is roughly equal to the number of vineyard regions in the world. To see what system would work best in our growing conditions, we did a lot of experimenting. At one point we had, someplace in the vineyard, just about every trellis system ever designed for cane-pruned vineyards. Each block, or section, of grapes had a different system. We started with an upright, three-wire trellis, in which the canes were tied to the first wire and the foliage to the second and third wires during the growing season. Then we tried a single-wire trellis because the logic of having the foliage hang from a high single wire, instead of being tied, seemed so smart. We didn't like the grape quality from the single-wire trellis, so we went to great expense to erect a complicated Geneva Double Curtain system, which created two trellises from one vine, separated by a four-foot cross arm. This was considered a good way to deal with vines that were especially vigorous, which ours were. I found the Geneva Double Curtain trellis a lot of work for inferior quality. We went back to our upright three-wire system because it was simplest and produced the best grapes. The only system I never tried was the one designed by Scott Henry for his vineyard near Roseburg, in southern Oregon. It had a double trellis, too, with one set trained upward and one set down.

We experimented with more than trellises. The experiment for which I had the highest hopes turned out to be our biggest failure. We got the idea of using geese in the vineyard when we heard they were used to weed the fields at mint farms—they ate the weeds and left the mint. I envisioned a pastoral scene with fat, happy geese wandering around the vineyard, feasting on weeds and leaving the vines to grow healthy and lush. Here was an idea that had everything going for it. It was more environmentally friendly than spraying herbicide or running equipment to mow or till, and it would save time and money. We chose a block of vines that we could fence relatively easily—three acres of Riesling adjacent to our house. We could watch the geese from our deck.

There were some immediate obstacles. We needed to fence, but we also needed to get a tractor up and down the rows to spray for mildew and botrytis (rot). We met this challenge with a makeshift chicken wire fence that had to be removed when we needed to spray, which was every ten to fourteen days all summer. But we figured all this extra time and energy was a small price to pay for such a great idea.

Two dozen white Chinese goslings arrived at our house in March. I had never had any farm animals and couldn't wait. When we opened the box, forty-eight tiny bright eyes looked up and gave us little goose smiles, accompanied by considerable twittering. We bonded immediately. They were so little that we put them in a small pen until they got bigger and we got the fencing in place. They came waddling, honking eagerly, whenever they saw or heard us. We chuckled at their antics.

In April, when the vines had not fully leafed out but the grass and weeds were growing fast and at their tender and tasty best, we embarked on our great experiment. As far as we knew, no other vineyard in Oregon had even thought of trying this. We put the geese in among the vines, in a section that has been known since as the Goosepen Block. The young geese loved their new freedom and wandered around giving all the various plants the taste test. I expected they would develop a taste for the leafy weeds. The vines would be too high for them to reach, anyway.

Our plan started to fall apart right away. The geese just wanted to be near us. When we went out onto the deck to see how they were doing, they'd come running over and line up along the fence, honking at us. When we weren't outside, they would sit quietly at the fence and wait for us to reappear. I tried going into the vineyard and showing them the far reaches of the block. They dutifully allowed me to herd them, and then they went back to their positions along the fence line facing our house. We thought maybe they would cover more of the block after they had eaten all the weeds in the section near the house. It never happened. They spent the rest of their lives trying to be near us, while the weeds grew freely.

We chose one pair to keep, and the rest ended up in our freezer. I cooked one, but we couldn't eat it. They stayed in the freezer for years. I was simply unable to bring myself to deal with them. It wasn't until we moved and I had to empty the freezer that I finally closed the chapter on the geese— except, that is, for the two goose-down pillows that Bill had given me for Christmas. For many years we laid our heads on the fluffy remains of our unwilling weed eaters.

The pair that we kept, dubbed Papa Goose and Gertie, grew large and elegant. They hung out in the front yard and liked to camp on the front doormat. The whole front porch was soon awash in goose poop. Not good. Wayne helped me fence in an area off our deck that became their pasture. We built a little pond and a house for them. I even bought a series of exotic ducks to keep Papa and Gertie company.

Our most successful vineyard experiment was far less glamorous: testing various grasses as potential cover crops between the grape rows to prevent erosion. Ours was one of a handful of vineyards that worked with the U.S. Soil Conservation Service and Oregon State University to test a variety of perennial and annual grasses. We later learned that the level of cooperation for this project was unprecedented. It was uncommon just to have two different departments at the university working together. My goal was to find a grass that would prevent erosion but would not compete with the vines for water, since our vineyard wasn't irrigated, and would be stalwart enough to withstand equipment driving over it. From among the eight different perennial grasses we tried, we identified a sheep fescue called Covar that did all those things and, in addition, never grew more than four inches high. I sowed that wonderful little grass as a cover crop on our whole vineyard, as did many other farmers.

The U.S. Soil Conservation Service recognized my work in 1984 by honoring Sokol Blosser as Cooperator of the Year for the Yamhill Soil and Water Conservation District. There was a dinner and a presentation at which I expected to be honored, but I might as well have been invisible. People looked right past me and came over to congratulate Bill and ask him about Sokol Blosser's project. They assumed the farmer and decision maker was the man, as of course it usually was among the local farmers. I took it as discrimination, no less upsetting for being unintended.

⁘

Before and during harvest, it was always a challenge to keep the wild birds away. Cedar waxwings and robins especially loved the ripening grapes. Cedar waxwings move in large flocks, flying like a squadron of small planes. Their elegant descent on the vineyard, in perfect formation, belied the damage they were about to do. I admired their grace and they were easy to scare, so it was hard to dislike them. But I came to hate robins. Plump and wily, the robins acted alone rather than in flocks, but there were many of them in the vineyard, and they ate a lot. They would hide in the leafy canopy when they saw us, and then go back to eating when we had gone. When I walked the vineyard with the dogs, Bagel and Muffin always took it as a personal affront when they saw birds in the vines and took off after them, barking ferociously. But their most energetic efforts did not solve the problem.

I hated and feared guns, but finally I learned to shoot to scare the birds. We had tried everything else: driving the pickup around honking the horn, riding bikes down the rows and yelling, tying a helium balloon with a picture of a hawk to a trellis wire, turning on an electronic device that emitted bird distress calls, shooting an air cannon. The cannons now operate off propane canisters, but they were more elaborate and difficult in the early days of our vineyard. The spark had to be ignited by gas that was generated when water dripped on carbide rocks in a sealed chamber. Maintaining those cannons was tough in Oregon's rainy fall season.

I would go out at the birds' feeding times—in the early morning and in the late afternoon—with my shotgun and my ear protection. I had a little off-road vehicle called a Hester ag truck that looked like a cross between a four-wheel ATV and a golf cart. It had big knobby tires to traverse the vineyards, a bench seat so two people could ride, and a three-foot-by-three-foot compartment behind the seat for supplies. When Alison was little, we went into the vineyard to scare birds every morning after the boys got on the school bus. I bundled her up and she sat in the supply compartment, holding onto the sides with both hands. We bounced up and down the vineyard rows, two fearless females protecting our crop. When it was time to stop and shoot, I put big earmuff protectors on her and popped the shotgun a few times. I rarely hit anything, but the noise scared the birds and I had the satisfaction of doing something about the bird problem.

Harvest season is always the most stressful time of year. The birds can eat the whole crop, the weather is changeable, and I am acutely aware that the future of the wines hinges on my picking decisions. Every year has its own twists and turns, but when I think of harvests, my mind always jumps to the disaster of 1984—the harvest from hell.

That year an unusually cold and wet spring had delayed bloom until mid July, almost a month late, so we knew harvest would also be later than normal. We would have to depend on Oregon's classic Indian summer to finish the ripening process. In early October, I walked the vineyard monitoring the grapes. Plump Pinot Noir clusters hung in neat rows along the fruiting canes. They had turned purple, but they were still tart and did not yet have the delicious multifaceted taste I knew they could acquire. We needed at least two more weeks of good weather. We never got it. Once the rain started, it didn't stop.

As the cold gray rain pelted the vineyard, I sat inside, frustrated, helpless, and miserable. I tried to keep myself busy, but all I could do was look out the window and worry, hoping that the next day our usual Indian summer was going to arrive. I passed the time by baking—and eating—cookies: chocolate chip, butterscotch chip, oatmeal. Between the rain and overeating, I was a colossal grouch.

Finally the rain stopped, and I went out to inspect the damage. It was still foggy, and a rain-forest dampness hung in the air. The ground was so soggy that I knew we couldn't get a tractor into the vineyard; it would have slid around on the hillside. The grapes tasted watery, their flavor diluted. By some miracle, they hadn't split. The forecast was for more rain. I couldn't believe it. What had happened to our Indian summer? We had always wondered which season was most important, and the consensus had been that they were equal in importance. The harvest of 1984 showed us that one season mattered most: Oregon's typically long, warm autumn was the secret to its great grapes.

I decided to pull in the harvest. When we brought in the Pinot Noir, it had absorbed so much water it was almost 40 percent heavier than we had forecast. I decided to take a chance and wait a little longer to bring in the last of Chardonnay. The weather never broke, and we harvested in the rain. I felt apologetic for the pickers who had to slosh uphill to the ends of the rows toting two buckets full of grapes, over thirty pounds each, since we couldn't get the tractor onto the steep slope at the lower end of the rows. We paid them extra to pick under those terrible conditions, and our picking contractor, Ofelia's husband, Frank De La Cruz, rewarded his crew with boxes of Kentucky Fried Chicken when they finished.

The wine reflected the watery harvest and we decided to declassify the vintage, meaning that we produced only a nonvintage Pinot Noir in 1984. The irony is that the 1983 and 1985 vintages were two of the best in Oregon's short history. I get a sinking feeling in my stomach every year that we get rain in September. A disaster like 1984 is always just a rainstorm away. When the sky is dark gray and the rain is coming down steadily, it's hard to imagine sunny weather returning. But it always has, except for that one year. The memory keeps me humble.

I worked enthusiastically with Wayne and the rest of the crew for seven years. We farmed the vineyard and the orchards, and then we planted more acres of grapes when we took the orchards out. We created a nursery and sold our grape cuttings to new vineyards arriving in the valley. We researched cover crops, pruning, trellising, and canopy management. With all that attention, the farm became profitable for the first time.

4

Growth

When our small group of local wineries decided to band together, in the early 1980s, to form the Yamhill County Winery Association, our first project was to host open houses at all the wineries during the three days after Thanksgiving. It became a wine country tradition, copied later by county winery groups all over the state.

The original nine wineries (Adelsheim, Amity, Arterberry, Chateau Benoit, Elk Cove, Erath, Eyrie, Hidden Springs, and Sokol Blosser) advertised together in Portland, Salem, and Seattle newspapers to lure people out to wine country. People were glad to get out of the house and show off Oregon's newest industry to visiting friends and relatives. As the number of participating wineries grew, so did the number of visitors and the popularity of wine touring.

"Wine Country Thanksgiving," as we called it, became our biggest retail weekend of the year. We started out welcoming visitors in the tasting room, and then moved into the winery cellar to handle the crowds. We served food, offered tastes of all our wines, lowered prices for the weekend, displayed holiday gift baskets, and brought in neighboring farmers to sell their chocolate-covered hazelnuts, flavored honey, marionberry preserves, and Christmas swags and wreaths. Holiday greens, wooden lattice, and bright red poinsettias helped mask the tanks, barrels, catwalks, and refrigeration pipe. Despite its no-frills wine-production layout, the winery had a festive feel.

The founding members of the Yamhill County Winery Association. Back row, left to right: Bill Blosser, Don Byard, Myron Redford, Dick Erath, Fred Arterberry, Fred Benoit, and David Lett. Front row, left to right: Joe Campbell and Dave Adelsheim. (Photo by Tom Ballard, 1983.)

We made it a family event. In the early years, Grandma Betty took charge of the tasting room kitchen, which was separated from the main space by a long counter on which she kept a large coffee urn for nondrinkers and designated drivers. She was adept at chatting with visitors while attending to her main job, slicing French bread to go with the cheese on the food platters. The crowds increased. When she got arm cramps from slicing baguettes, she showed up with a gift for the winery—an electric bread slicer. Grandpa John helped pour wine, stopping occasionally to chat with former patients who were delighted to see one of their favorite doctors.

Usually they wanted to hang out at John's table and talk, and we sometimes had to rescue him to keep the tasting line from backing up.

Nik, Alex, and Alison did whatever they were able to do, making change at the admissions table as soon as they were old enough, and later, when they were older and stronger, restocking wine, washing glasses, and carrying cases out for customers. Besides providing valuable help, they earned the "big money" they used to buy family Christmas and birthday presents. In the first years, before we had a full-time bookkeeper, we made a custom each night of counting the day's take. We brought the small gray metal cash box home and gave the kids the honor of doing the counting. They sat on the floor in the living room and learned, at an early age, how to put the bills in order, all facing the same way, how to count the change, and how to fill out the cash-box records.

Sometimes I wondered what it would be like to go away for the Thanksgiving holidays, or to be free for shopping or whatever we felt like doing. It wasn't an option. Wine Country Thanksgiving was too important to our business, so we rallied the family and tried to make it fun.

We were always on the lookout for vineyard or winery projects we could tackle as a family so the kids could be involved. One year Grandma Betty showed us an advertisement in a Christmas catalog for a package of shredded grapevines to be used as smoke flavoring for the grill. She brought it as a curiosity, but teenage Nik seized on the idea immediately, and NGB (his initials) Enterprises was born. He tackled the production side, and I agreed to help with the packaging. We would sell it in the tasting room.

Production started that February, as Nik and Alex (NGB Enterprises' first employee) pulled the vine prunings out of the vineyard rows. They kept the Pinot Noir and Chardonnay separate and transported the big piles of prunings down to the shed to dry out. Nik bought a shredder to grind the prunings to the right consistency. The shredded prunings, which we called Grapevine Smoke, dried in wooden totes until the family (free labor) could get together to bag, seal, and label our new product.

The packaging was more involved than I had intended, mainly because I got carried away. I pictured people grilling with Pinot Noir Grapevine Smoke and then drinking Pinot Noir with their meal, so I wanted to package the smoke and the wine together, in a two-bottle wine box. This required putting the new product in a long, narrow, special-order plastic bag that, when filled, would be about the size of a wine bottle. And if there was to be a card for the directions (simple: soak in water before putting over the coals on the grill), why not print recipes on the other side? I found a woman to create recipes for both the Pinot Noir and the Chardonnay. When she tried out the two different Grapevine Smoke samples, she called to say, "I never would have guessed how striking the taste difference was between the Pinot Noir and Chardonnay smoke. It's amazing!"

The final step was to have a colorful label designed and printed. I spent more time on this project than I had intended and did all the running around, since Nik was not old enough to drive. But I enjoyed the challenge. We sold the individual bags in the tasting room and made up gift boxes with the wine and matching Grapevine Smoke.

The next year we decided to offer our new product to Norm Thompson, a Portland catalog company whose slogan was Escape from the Ordinary. Nik and I visited the Norm Thompson headquarters to pitch the new package we had devised—a slatted wooden crate containing one bag each of Pinot Noir Grapevine Smoke and Chardonnay Grapevine Smoke shrink-wrapped so that the products, labels, and recipe cards were clearly visible. To our delight, their buyer, Emily Crumpacker, loved it and ordered a thousand boxes. In the manner of small-world stories, Emily resurfaced in my life years later as the editor who published my short vineyard memoir in the *Oregon Historical Society* magazine and encouraged me to keep going and write a book.

We had made only a hundred bags of each smoke the first year. In our excitement, Nik and I ignored the logistics of increasing production by a factor of ten and jumped at the chance to be in the prestigious Norm Thompson catalog. Production went into high gear. Every weekend the family gathered in the equipment shed and chatted as we whittled away at the mounds of material in the totes. As the rain pounded on the metal shed roof, we ran our little assembly line and managed to keep our good humor, as long as we could see progress. I put the labels on the bags. Grandma Betty, Grandpa John, and Nik, in white dust masks, did the bagging. Bill ran the temperamental hot sealer to close the bags. Alex put the bags in the crates so they could go to Portland for shrink-wrapping. Alison was too little to do much but play and get in the way. The final product was impressive; we were proud to see it in the catalog, but nobody was willing to do it again.

⁂

The Newport (Oregon) Seafood and Wine Festival each February was another family event. The Newport Chamber of Commerce started the festival in the early 1980s to lure people to the coast during the winter, and we supported it for many years. Bill's folks went along. John helped us pour wine while Betty took the kids—to the aquarium, the wax museum, the hotel pool, and the beach. I know her job was harder than ours was. Every morning, before the festival started, we all went out for poppy-seed pancakes. It was as close to vacation as we got for many years.

With all the tastings, festivals, and wine dinners, we ran out of time and energy for any other social life. But we always took time for family.

Besides holidays and birthday celebrations, we had regular breakfasts and dinners with Bill's parents and with mine after they moved to McMinnville in 1980. I had not known any of my grandparents and never knew what I had missed until I saw how much Bill's parents and mine enriched our kids' lives. My kids knew all four of their grandparents, stayed with them occasionally, and looked forward to being with them.

My mother, Phyllis, was the kind of person I would choose for a friend. Outgoing and opinionated, she was a woman with a lively and cultured intellect, imparting her views frankly and authoritatively. As her friend, I would have laughed when we disagreed. But being a daughter is a different playing field. I always took her criticism seriously—too seriously, I now know. She never hesitated to point out my faults or mistakes she saw me making. If one of my kids did something she didn't approve of—was too clingy, interrupted someone, fussed at the dinner table—she would point it out, along with an example of someone whose kids were always well-behaved, usually one of my brothers. If she didn't like my hair or my outfit, she said so. She thought she was just helping me be a better person, but it felt as if she were always telling me what to do. Her constant judgment and advice made me feel inadequate or stupid, or both. When I needed comfort, I went to Betty Blosser.

How lucky I was to have a mother-in-law who reversed the stereotype by being unfailingly encouraging and supportive. I could never decide whether she simply didn't see the things my mother was criticizing or saw them and just chose a positive approach. Betty Blosser may not really have thought I was the best thing to happen to her son, but she always treated me as though she did. She was intuitive about how people were feeling and what they needed. One year when Bill was out of town for my birthday and I was feeling forlorn and forgotten, she drove out, scooped up me and the kids, and took us out for a birthday dinner. It cheered me immensely and was typical of her thoughtfulness. She had a knack for giving just the right present and continually amazed me with gifts I loved and hadn't thought of asking for. How did she know these things? She would call me before Christmas to ask, "Do you think Nik is ready for his own tool set [or wagon or bicycle]?" Her ideas always entailed something that would encourage activity, motor skills, and creativity. Occasionally she went over the top— like the Christmas she gave Nik and Alex yellow hard hats with built-in sirens and flashing lights on top. She was smart enough not to ask me in advance about those. The kids loved them.

Bill's dad, John Blosser, not only was a good orthopedic surgeon, but was also open to alternative medicine before most MDs would even admit it existed. His patients adored him, judging from the number of thank-you letters and Christmas gifts he received. He developed a reputation in the medical community for using "radical" methods that worked, and he gave workshops to MDs on spinal manipulation. He later got interested in cranial manipulation and Chinese medicine and, after a trip to China, included aspects of these in his workshops. At family get-togethers, we all looked forward to having John give us a "tune-up." He bought a folding massage table for these occasions, decided it was too awkward, and built a better one. After the holiday or birthday dinner, someone would drag out John's table, and the ten or so of us would wait our turns. John accepted his role with an air of proud resignation, but he was very skilled and I believe he would have been disappointed to miss his chance to perform.

Bill and his father were at their best when they were working on a project together, and, fortunately for their relationship, there seemed to be an inexhaustible supply of those. They didn't hesitate to take on big projects. One year they installed a fireplace in our house. Another year they built a twenty-foot flight of stairs off our deck.

A family picnic at the winery. Alex and I are standing at the back. Seated in front of us, left to right, are my father and mother, Gus and Phyllis Sokol; and Bill's father, John Blosser. In the front row, left to right, are Bill, Alison, Nik, and Bill's mother, Betty Blosser. The photo was taken in 1986, when my father was entering the advanced stages of Alzheimer's disease. (Photo by Tom Ballard.)

My family, the Sokols, were older and lived farther from the winery, so their main involvement was financial. When we got together with Bill's family, we laughed and had fun. When we were with my family, we had serious discussions about winery finance. The kids enjoyed being with Grandma Phyllis and Grandpa Gus when they moved to McMinnville, but for me the financial issues always hovered in the background.

After talking my brothers into investing and getting the winery started, my father faded into the background. Years later, we realized he had been entering the early stages of Alzheimer's—the disease that would turn my funny, vibrant father into an empty shell of a person. As my father ceded his leadership role, my brothers, who had never been enthusiastic about the winery, became reluctant and demanding investors. Ronnie, the youngest of the three, took Dad's place as the strategist and power broker. He lived in France, but even from a distance he exerted decisive influence. My mother and father trusted him totally and accepted his judgment on everything. As an attorney who had done major legal and financial work for my father's business, he saw himself as the protector of the family's investment.

Bill's ten-year financial forecasts, which had seemed conservative and reasonable at the time, predicted profitability in five years, by 1982. We weren't even close. That was partly because we had used California numbers. Wine from Napa was a known quantity. When we went on sales trips, the first response became sadly predictable: "Oregon? I didn't know you could make wine there!" People east of the Rocky Mountains didn't even know where Oregon was.

With no big advertising campaign, we had to attract customers one at a time, meeting them and encouraging them to try our wine. For a few years, we were one of only two or three Oregon wineries with any national distribution. We started national sales with a well-known Burgundy importer, Robert Haas, who confessed, when we first met him in the late 1970s, that he hadn't yet tasted a domestic Pinot Noir he liked. We watched his face as he tasted ours, and when he started nodding as he swirled it in his mouth, we smiled with relief. Bob Haas's firm, Vineyard Brands, placed our wine across the country in boutique wine stores and expensive restaurants. We were thrilled. But we quickly learned that an Oregon wine had no cachet in Manhattan, Boston, Washington, D.C., or Chicago. It sat on the shelves.

In the mid 1980s, Stephen Cary started a marketing group to promote Oregon wines nationally, and the added exposure helped. But it was a long, slow process.

The general economic recession of the early 1980s dealt us a double whammy by depressing what sales we did have while simultaneously inflating interest rates. As president of the winery, Bill bore the brunt of the criticism from the Sokol family members who comprised the board of directors. Although they recognized that the economy was in recession, my brothers felt misled because things hadn't turned out as Bill had predicted. The implication was that if Bill had done a better job, the winery would be profitable. We were constantly on the defensive. It was a painful partnership for me, caught between my family and Bill. I had never been assertive with my older brothers and was easily shot down when I tried to defend Bill. And because this was my family, I couldn't feel the unmitigated rage that Bill felt at our predicament.

One reason the recession hit us so hard was that we were financed almost entirely by debt. Bill and I had lobbied hard and succeeded in convincing the head of U.S. Bank in McMinnville that we should get a Small Business Administration (SBA) loan—almost unheard of for a winery at that time. Procuring the SBA loan ourselves, without having to rely on my father, had been an important step in freeing up the Sokol family money. It had taken mountains of paperwork, but it had been worth it. We thought we had a great deal with an interest rate of 3 percent over prime, but when prime escalated from 7 percent to 18 percent, we choked on the payments. We were paying 21 percent interest on most of our debt.

Close to panic, we knew we needed to do something fast. The family bailed us out. We were able to pay off our ill-fated SBA loan by borrowing from a retirement plan my father, under Ronnie's guidance, had set up for my mother. While it saved the winery from going under, it only made matters worse with the family. We knew that somehow, as soon as we could, we had to relieve the Sokol family of winery ownership. We tried not to let tensions over business and finance get in the way of our family life or the kids' relations with their grandparents, but it was on our minds constantly, and it was hard to keep the discomfort hidden.

⁘

Enjoying our kids helped us, at least temporarily, forget the business problems. We made a point of having dinner together, and on winter evenings we played Uno or Monopoly, built Lego trucks and spacecraft, did jigsaw puzzles, or read stories aloud. When Bill read *Charlie and the Chocolate Factory,* one chapter each night, we all claimed favorite listening spots and looked forward to the next installment. Shel Silverstein's poems were another favorite, especially the one about Sarah Cynthia Sylvia Stout, who wouldn't take the garbage out. The kids, who by then had chores, could relate to that tale.

When I started working in the vineyard full-time, Bill and I took responsibility alternate weeks for making dinners, and the boys had rotating chore assignments. Doing dishes and taking out garbage was one chore; washing, folding laundry, and setting the table was another. The rotation was posted on the refrigerator to take care of any "Oh, was this my week to set the table?" excuses. When we began, Alex had to stand on a chair to do the dishes. Later, Alison was added to the chore list, and the boys were allowed to cook dinner.

Enforcing the chores took a great deal of effort, including nagging, bribing, and demonstrating the consequences of failure. We kept at it and, for the most part, it worked. As teenagers, Nik and Alex composed a two-page mathematical calculation proving that we had worked them so ruthlessly that they had only two free hours a week. They presented it to us with great glee, showing no signs of being downtrodden.

❖

With my training and interest in education, I started worrying, when Nik was still in diapers, about how good the school system was in our rural district. I attended budget committee meetings to get an idea of the school administration's priorities. After a short stint on the committee, I was elected to the school board. All but one of the other board members were men—prominent local farmers who spoke with authority but, I came to realize, really had no idea what they were doing. I served two terms over eight years, facing the same thorny policy and funding issues local school boards deal with everywhere. Our board hired two new superintendents, struggled annually to convince the voters to fund the school programs, implemented a Spanish-English bilingual program, tried to supplement the academic program for gifted students, and dealt with community turmoil over sex education in the schools and the salacious language in library books, the latter controversy having been triggered by the profanity in John Steinbeck's *Of Mice and Men*.

The school district, which covered fifty-nine square miles, contained only two hundred students. Kindergarten through grade twelve were housed in two red brick buildings a quarter-mile apart along Ferry Street, the town's main drag. The grade-school building also contained the administrative offices. The junior high–high school had a berry field in front and a football field, encircled by a dirt track, in back. A large percentage of the students qualified for the free lunch program. The student body was not ethnically diverse, primarily Caucasian with about 20 percent Hispanic. The whole community turned out to cheer for sports, especially their state champion football team. Finishing high school was the goal for most students. Only a few went on to four-year colleges.

Long before he was tested, we suspected Nik would soon be bored by the meager supplemental programs that Dayton could afford to offer. It didn't seem like a big deal that he was reading in kindergarten, but it did cross my mind that it might be unusual for him to amuse himself when he stayed home sick from school by reading the encyclopedia and our small library of Time-Life science books. One night when Nik was still in elementary school, perhaps fourth grade, I came home from a school board meeting to find the house entirely dark and silent. I was startled to discover Bill sitting like a statue in the living room. "What happened?" I asked anxiously.

Out of the darkness came his answer: "Nik beat me at chess."

We found opportunities for Nik to supplement his rural schooling and were rewarded when it was time for college and he was accepted by both Princeton and Stanford. After anguished indecision, he opted for Stanford, trusting that if it were good enough for his parents, it would be good for him too.

As the second child, Alex had to find his own niche. Not doing his chores helped him find it. When he was about ten, he missed the morning school bus because Bill had made him finish washing the dishes, which he had failed to do the night before. I had been out in the vineyard and returned to find Alex crying. "Mom," he pleaded, "drive me to school. I can't walk. I'm going to be late." My heart went out to him, but I knew I had to back up Bill. I suggested he ride his bike. Off he went down the hill, one miserable little boy, scared to go all alone, knowing he would have to cross a busy state highway in the course of the four-mile ride.

I was watching for him when he pedaled into the driveway later that afternoon. "Mom," he panted after navigating our steep hill, "I did it! It wasn't so bad." He stopped and then announced triumphantly, "I think I'll ride my bike again tomorrow." That summer he joined a bicycle club and took long rides every weekend. At twelve he joined a racing team and got an underage work permit so he could repair bikes part-time at Tommy's Bike Shop in McMinnville. As a teenager, his specialty was track racing on the velodrome. At his peak during the summer, he spent all his waking hours working at a bike shop, racing, working out, or eating. We would go out for a big family dinner and come home stuffed, but Alex would go straight to the cereal cabinet for more. He seemed to be solid muscle, and it was impossible to fill him up. I asked John Rizzo, a professional photographer who had done work for the winery, to photograph Alex at a race. I imagined Alex, someday in the future, patting his expanded girth and showing his kids this picture of his past glory. I wonder what would have happened if I'd given in and driven him to school that day.

•••

Bill tolerated my ducks, geese, peacock, and dogs, but he finally got so fed up with the cat hair and mouse guts that he unilaterally declared that our three cats had to stay outside or in the basement. Faced with the hard evidence, I had to agree that the cat hair and miscellaneous small rodent parts were a problem and the house would be cleaner if it were catless. Then YumYum came on the scene.

I was at the vet's getting more pills for Bagel and telling him about Pud, our butterscotch male cat recently run over by a gravel truck. He told me a kitten with a mangled foreleg had just been left on his doorstep. He thought he probably should put her to sleep, but she was so cute he couldn't bear to do it. Would I take the kitten if he did the surgery to remove her leg? He brought her out for me to see. She was small and light gray with some striping, big blue eyes, and a foreleg that dangled oddly. Without hesitation I said yes, so enamored with this beautiful, unfortunate kitten that I totally forgot the new cat rule. Clearly, a three-legged kitten would have to stay inside.

Bill was not pleased to see me come home with this kitten and violate the new policy so quickly, but he got a lot of mileage out of the episode, lamenting to family and friends the lengths to which I was prepared to go to have a cat in the house. He nicknamed her Tripod, and I knew I'd better come up with something fast or she would be Tripod forever. Alex saved the day.

He had named a cat once before. When he was about six, Alex and I went down to Ted and Verni's to choose a kitten from their new litter. We chose a long-legged, unusually elegant coal-black kitten. Alex pronounced the new kitten "Freddie." I couldn't talk him out of his choice. I still laugh when I think of that beautiful, sleek kitten being named Freddie.

Alex was a teenager when I brought home our new, three-legged kitten. We had recently been to Portland to see a live performance of *The Mikado*. Alex loved the songs, especially the one about the Lord High Executioner. He went around the house singing "I Have a Little List" until we were ready to muzzle him. With *The Mikado* fully occupying his brain, he came up with the best female name he could, YumYum. YumYum had just the right ring, and our new kitten no longer had to put up with the indignity of a name that called attention to her disability.

YumYum's feisty spirit and can-do approach to life inspired us all. More than once I saw her scare a four-legged cat with a ferocious growl. One of us would start to complain about some hardship, but then look at YumYum, who lived with significant hardship and didn't seem to be complaining at all, and shut up. She showed us that handicap was a state of mind—one she didn't have. YumYum stayed with me for seventeen years, through numerous trials and tribulations. When she died, it was the end of an era for me. Papa Goose, Vern the peacock, Muffin, Bagel, Caddie, YumYum— all those pets added color, humor, and comfort over the years. Without them, our lives would have been leaner.

⋮

In 1986, as my time on the Dayton School Board was about to end, I was approached by a friend active in the Yamhill County Democratic Party. The local Democrats were looking for someone to run for the Oregon House of Representatives. He gave me his sales pitch, telling me the legislature needed another woman, especially one like me with both business and farming background. Of course, the party would help me with money, expertise, and volunteers. He flattered me, and he made it sound much easier than it turned out to be.

Oregon has what it likes to call a "citizen legislature," elected members who are not professional politicians, but part of the job-holding citizenry. The two branches, Senate and House, meet in full session every other year, usually for about six months, and in between the members spent time connecting with their constituency, raising money for the next campaign, and meeting to plan legislation for the next session. House members' terms are two years, senators' are four. The incumbent from my district intended to run again, so I would have an uphill race against someone whose name was familiar to voters, and who knew how to work the system. On the other hand, he had not had much competition in the previous election and had become complacent and ineffective.

I wasn't sure I wanted to get into politics, because I hadn't been impressed with politicians as a group. But I remembered Senator Nancy Ryles, who had helped us with the TODS signage, navigating so honorably through the legislative labyrinth. Her example encouraged me; the invitation appealed to my vanity; the challenge appealed to my competitiveness. Could I take time off to campaign and to serve in the legislature if I were elected? Did I have the energy to organize and undergo a campaign?

Bill was running the winery. I had been working in the vineyard for six years and thought I could take some time off. I was a farmer and could bring that point of view to potential legislation; my involvement with the winery gave me the small-business perspective, and my school-board experience had given me some understanding of the shortcomings of the state school system. No legislators I knew could boast such breadth of experience. Bill encouraged me to go for it. That was the extra push I needed.

I assembled a campaign committee in the early spring, drawing on friends from the AAUW, McMinnville, and Linfield College, many of whom had some political experience. Jann Tankersley headed the steering committee composed of John Dillin, Walt Gowell, and Marylou Henry. Concerned enough about our community to be active, they were bright, strategic thinkers and committed to helping me get to the legislature. The primary election would be in May, the final election in November 1986.

My campaign brochure pictured me with local farmers, like Ted and Verni; with local businesspeople; and with my family. I walked or rode in every local parade and spoke to every local club I could get in front of. I visited retirement homes and walked the district, knocking on doors to introduce myself. My campaign committee put up lawn signs, sent out mailings, telephoned lists of registered voters. We had a great response, and I was very encouraged. We thought we might pull it off and I would be the first Democrat in memory to be elected from that district.

In the end, I couldn't compete with the advantages of incumbency. Lobbyists were afraid to take a chance on me and gave their money and support to the incumbent. I was especially disappointed not to get the support

I waved to the crowds from the back of a mint-condition vintage automobile in the 1986 St. Paul Fourth of July parade. It was one of many parades in which I walked or rode that summer.

of either the farm or the school lobby. The incumbent's extra money allowed him to put out a campaign piece that appeared in mailboxes the Saturday before the final election, timed to leave me no opportunity to respond. It was a "hit piece" implying that since I owned a winery, I would be soft on drunk driving, whereas he, the incumbent, had a track record of being tough. It was cleverly worded to raise doubts without directly accusing and provided the extra margin needed to put him over the top. I was terribly disappointed, but we came close, and I felt good about the campaign we had run.

Two years later I ran again, this time for the Oregon Senate, against the brother of the incumbent who had defeated me for the House seat. This second campaign took on enormous emotional significance. In 1986,

I only thought my opponent was ineffectual. But my opponent in 1988 stood for everything I was against, and my campaign felt like a crusade. He was a member of the religious right and had led Oregon's Right to Life movement. He homeschooled his children and had no experience with the public school system. He promoted antihomosexual legislation. He had never held public office and hadn't paid his property taxes for years. I was running for an open seat, and at a Democratic candidate-training workshop, one of the senior Democratic senators looked down at me and declared, with a pomposity that gave me goose bumps, "This election is yours to lose."

I knew that to win in my district I would need Republican as well as Democratic support. Penny Durant, my vineyard neighbor and friend and a longtime Republican, agreed to run my campaign, and she made it a truly great one. I secured the endorsement of every Republican-leaning newspaper in my district. I had billboards throughout the district. Governor Neil Goldschmidt spent a day campaigning with me, as did Les Au Coin and Ron Wyden, the two congressional representatives whose districts overlapped mine. Moderate Republicans rallied for me. The Oregon teachers union paid one of its interns to help with my campaign, conducted polling, and helped with strategy. Most of the lobbies endorsed me and gave me money. The Oregon Women's Political Caucus, however, refused to back me after I told its members I had doubts about allowing underage girls to get abortions without notifying their parents. I was running against their nemesis, but they withheld support because I wouldn't accept 100 percent of their platform. I was deeply hurt that my natural allies—progressive women—wouldn't support me. The Women's Political Caucus was neither well-funded nor powerful, so their rejection had little practical impact. But I was perplexed by their bizarre, and ultimately self-destructive, position.

A pleasanter surprise was the support I received from the sisters in the convent at Mount Angel, a small Catholic farming community in the district. They were active in helping farmworkers, as was I. One told me, "I know we disagree on abortion, but we agree on so many other issues that we will vote for you."

Abortion and homosexuality were big issues in the campaign. I went to meetings ready to talk about education and farming, and the audience just wanted my views on those two hot-button topics. The first question was always "Are you in favor of abortion?" and the second, "Would you want your children taught by a homosexual teacher?" I was amazed at the level of emotion that accompanied those questions.

I believed strongly that a woman, not a government (especially one run by men), should be the decision maker about her body, but I really resented having the issue defined in a way that forced people to take sides. The issue really was unwanted babies, and the solution should have focused on birth control. Nobody is pro-abortion; abortion is an after-the-fact attempt to rectify an unacceptable situation. If these two groups had put their combined energies into birth-control education, or even abstinence advocacy, they could have accomplished something significant. Instead, they staked out territory, flung accusations, and divided the populace, diverting attention from the real issue.

The Farm Bureau also denied me an endorsement, probably because of my environmental advocacy. As one friend reflected, "The Farm Bureau never met a chemical it didn't like." But I felt I had all the good people behind me. I did lack the name familiarity that my opponent acquired by way of his brother, who had been on the ballot for many years. Even though my opponent had never held office, the recognizable surname gave him an incumbent's advantage.

My opponent put out a last-minute mailer accusing me of endorsing homosexuality, but we thought we could weather it. We were worn out from the long, emotional campaign, but the polls showed me ahead. Bill, Alex, and I went to my election-night party at Nick's Italian Cafe in McMinnville ready to celebrate. The restaurant was full of people who had worked on my campaign, and we stood around making small talk, hardly touching the food and wine, waiting for the results. The first numbers showed me trailing. Don't worry, people said, your strong areas haven't been tallied yet. But I never caught up. Bill concluded I had lost midway through the evening and asked if I minded if he left. My insides were numb as defeat edged closer, and I couldn't believe he would leave me to face it all alone. I wanted him to hold and comfort me, but I knew he felt bad. I told him to go ahead, but I felt as if I'd been hit while I was down.

I would gladly have curled up in a dark closet and had a good cry. For the sake of my supporters, I stayed until the end, determined to lose gracefully. Seventeen-year-old Nik, who had been active in the campaign, stayed with me and drove me home. I was so grateful for his presence. I felt empty. Not only to have lost, but to have lost to someone who was totally unqualified and who stood for everything I was against, was a piercing blow. How could I have lost to this person? What was wrong with me? All those volunteers had believed in me, had spent time and money on my campaign, and I had lost and let them down. The words of the older senator came back to haunt me — the campaign had been mine to lose, and I had lost it.

The seasoned politicos argued over how it had happened and how the polling could have been so wrong. In the end, the consensus was that there were enough reasons for various segments of the population in my very conservative district to vote against me: I was not against homosexuality or abortion, I was a woman, and my business produced an alcoholic beverage. Knowing what had happened didn't help. I had had faith in the voters and the democratic process; as a student of American history, perhaps I should have known better.

I sank into a depression, which the counselor called a "grieving process," that only time would heal. As the gloom of winter settled in, I sat on the living room floor with my back against the couch and played solitaire for hours, replaying the campaign in my mind. Penny cleaned up the campaign details.

One morning, as he was leaving for school, Alex asked me earnestly if I'd found the silver lining yet. His question was so sweet that I wanted to smile, but tears came instead. I knew I just had to keep going. The crew hadn't started yet, but I went out into the vineyard to prune.

The Oregon industry continued to grow, and by the mid 1980s there were four thousand acres of wine grapes planted and fifty Oregon wineries. Interest in Oregon wine was still in its infancy, though. On sales trips, I still carried a map so that I could point out Oregon as the state north of California. But in September 1985, a special promotion set up by the Oregon Wine Advisory Board (WAB) sparked national interest in Oregon Pinot Noir.

Oregon's WAB had been created by the legislature in 1984, at the urging of Oregon winegrowers, to do wine marketing and wine-grape research. Its funding came from the industry, in the form of a small gallonage tax on bottled wine and a per-ton tax on Oregon grapes. The WAB policy-making board, selected by the director of the Oregon Department of Agriculture, was composed of vineyard and winery people from the major wine areas in the state. Bill was one of the first board members.

The board gave the responsibility for wine-grape research to Oregon State University's Food Science and Horticulture Departments, creating a focus on grapes and wine that had, until then, been negligible at the university. Members of WAB directed the marketing side themselves, hiring outside public-relations people to help. One of the first ploys of their new public-relations consultant, Fred Delkin, was to set up a special tasting of Oregon Pinot Noir in New York City. This was the first time the Oregon wineries had joined to promote themselves on a national scale.

It couldn't have come at a better time. In late August and early September 1985, as the grapes were ripening, Bill and I started wondering whether we should even bother to harvest our Pinot Noir. Selling Pinot Noir was such a struggle. It was priced at $7.95 a bottle, and we figured we had a three-year supply at the current rate of sales. While we were considering our options, Bill went off to New York for the big tasting.

Fred had convinced the International Wine Center in New York City to host a taste-off between French Burgundy and Oregon Pinot Noir of the 1983 vintage. About ten top-growth Burgundies and fifteen of the best Oregon Pinot Noirs were selected for tasting. Invitations went out to all the top sommeliers, wine retailers, and wine writers in the New York area. It would be a blind tasting, and that idea was seductive to people who prided themselves on their discriminating palates. The event was well attended. Attendees were asked to taste, indicate whether they thought each wine was from Burgundy or Oregon, and then rank their top five favorites.

Any betting person would have put money on a French sweep. The bet would have lost. To the astonishment of the tasters, when the truth was revealed, the top five favorites were all from Oregon. Both of the top two had been made at Sokol Blosser, one for us and the other for another winery just getting started, Yamhill Valley Vineyards. The tasters had the grace to admit that they simply could not distinguish the French Burgundy from the Oregon Pinot Noir. The buzz could be heard from coast to coast.

The phones at the winery started ringing, and we sold out of our three-year supply of Pinot Noir in three months. There was no question about going ahead with the harvest, and a good thing too. The 1985 vintage ranks as one of Oregon's greatest. I still dream about Sokol Blosser's 1985 Red Hills Pinot Noir, though it is long gone and I haven't tasted it in years. It combined in a magnificent way two qualities I love in a Pinot Noir, earth and elegance.

After that 1985 event, the wine world sharpened its focus on Oregon. Wine-tasting groups all over the country re-created the New York City tasting to prove to themselves that Oregon's showing in New York was not a fluke. It wasn't. Groups in Chicago, Washington, D.C., Detroit, Dallas, Atlanta, St. Louis, Seattle, and San Francisco ordered wine, held tastings, and reported similar results.

Unfortunately, Oregon's reputation did not climb steadily upward. The 1984 vintage, the one the wine world eagerly awaited after the lauded 1983 vintage quickly sold out, was a disaster. Many concluded that the success of Oregon's 1983 vintage was just a lucky one-time shot. The stellar 1985 vintage was very well received, and Oregon's fragile reputation started rebuilding.

Then came the '86 and '87 vintages, mediocre but promoted by Oregon's new marketing agent as fabulous. What a colossal mistake. Wine media and wine buyers were insulted, and Oregon's wine industry suffered damage to its credibility and reputation that took years to repair.

Enough interest in Pinot Noir had been generated to make possible a new Oregon event, the International Pinot Noir Celebration in McMinnville. The IPNC, as it came to be called, demonstrates how much can be accomplished when people work together and don't worry about who gets the credit. The first IPNC took place on the Linfield College campus August 7–9, 1987. On the tenth anniversary of IPNC, in 1997, people tried to recall how it started, and everybody had a slightly different version. This suggests two things: First, the creation of the IPNC represented the convergence of several ideas that gained momentum at the same time. Second, there were so many key players that no one person was pivotal. Here's my version.

By 1985, the wine industry had become prominent enough that community groups and chambers of commerce were looking for ways to use it to promote their interests. As the largest town in the area, with the most active civic groups, McMinnville got the prize. Preliminary financing for the IPNC came from a locally high-powered group of businessmen—the past presidents of the McMinnville Chamber of Commerce—who saw the event as an economic development project to promote their city. The McMinnville Downtown Association wanted to help because it saw opportunity within the event to promote the historic downtown. The local wineries were willing to be involved because the event positioned them well, too. Even the state of Oregon got involved by providing an economic development grant to promote the Oregon wine industry and help the local economy. The genius of the project was in how well the event, which focused on a single wine and wasn't, after all, really international, was thought through and positioned.

Only the principals—the owners or winemakers—from the best Pinot Noir wineries all over the world, but especially from Burgundy, California, and Oregon, would be invited to show their wines. It would be a celebration, with camaraderie, not a competition. We would bring in famous chefs to create fabulous meals to go with Pinot Noir. The program would include tastings and seminars—enough education to make serious wine drinkers happy but not so much as to deaden the mood—as well as four- and five-course luncheons and dinners. Attendees would be an equal mix of wine-aficionado consumers and members of the wine trade. The event would be limited to about 350 attendees and 100 winery principals, so that attendees could have quality time with the winery owners and winemakers.

We knew the concept was good. But before offering it to the public, we had to convince the right wineries from California and Burgundy to participate. We put together an honorary board so we could list their names, which were well known, instead of ours, which weren't, on our stationery. People like English wine writer Serena Sutcliffe, Oregon governor Neil Goldschmidt, and Robert Drouhin, a prominent Burgundian wine figure, agreed to help us by lending their names. Then the local winemakers who had contacts in California and abroad prevailed on their cohorts to partic- ipate. The original idea was to make the event truly international by rotat- ing the venue among Oregon, France, and California. But after the first few years, both the California and the Burgundian participants told us we should keep it in Oregon: they weren't up to the organizational challenge it presented.

As the planning progressed in 1986, I became convinced that the IPNC board would sink under the weight of its plans if it didn't have help. I offered to organize the event if the organization would pay me. The board agreed, and the McMinnville Chamber of Commerce gave me office space in its unused basement. The International Pinot Noir Celebration could say it had an office and a staff, but volunteers virtually ran the event for almost ten years. Judging by the people who volunteered, the whole McMinnville community was involved. Attendees at the early IPNCs never realized they were being served dinner and having their water glasses filled by McMinnville's mayor, bank president, and fire chief, as well as the county sheriff. The first IPNC board chairman was the head of the local Hewlett- Packard plant, and it was Hewlett-Packard engineers who devised the logis- tics for moving the correct portions of the two hundred cases of wine to various campus destinations for tastings, workshops, and meals.

The event grew into its name, and after a few years we no longer needed an honorary board to give us credibility. The IPNC played a crucial role for the industry by bringing the right people to Oregon wine country and positioning Oregon as a mecca for Pinot Noir lovers. Over the years, the board of directors considered enlarging the event, moving it to another venue, or duplicating it and taking it on the road. None of these things happened. It remained a low-key event on a little college campus in Mc-Minnville, Oregon, where attendees rubbed elbows with winemakers and the food and wine were otherworldly.

One of the key players in developing the IPNC concept and directing its emphasis toward food as well as wine was Nick Peirano, whose local restaurant played an important role in my life from the time it opened. Nick's Italian Cafe served as an oasis for Bill and me, while also educating our palates by introducing us to authentic Northern Italian cuisine. Nick's, as it came to be known, opened in McMinnville in 1977, the year of Sokol Blosser's first vintage. Started by two friends, Nick Peirano and John West, it was ahead of its time and an oddity in McMinnville, where the 1977 restaurant roster included Oriental Gardens, the Blue Moon tavern, Tommy's Coffee Shop, and the counter at Thrifty Drug. The fast-food giants hadn't yet discovered the area, but there were no white-tablecloth restaurants either. Nick and John took over an old coffee shop, Cafe Dinette, but didn't have the funds to do more than paint the interior. So we sat in worn turquoise plastic booths or at the counter on low, backless bar stools and ate exquisite food. I remember how excited we were for Nick when he was able to replace the turquoise plastic with more upscale brown Naugahyde.

Going to Nick's for dinner became the prize Bill and I awarded ourselves for surviving another month. It was always just the two of us, and our evening's entertainment was working our way through the prix fixe menu of five courses. From the moment we opened the door and were enveloped in the scent of roasted garlic and fresh bread to the last luscious mouthful of chocolate-hazelnut torte, Nick's was a familiar and well-loved ritual. Dinner there was an occasion for the two of us to talk about things that mattered, to lay out strategies for the winery, to talk about the kids, and just to be together. We made more than a few key decisions over dinner at Nick's.

Over the years, Nick's played a significant role in our culinary education. Julia Child had introduced us to gourmet cooking, and we had been to fancy restaurants around the country. But it was a revelation to dine in a restaurant that served exquisite food like this without being expensive or pretentious. Northern Italian cuisine wasn't yet popular, and the Italian restaurants we knew specialized in spaghetti with giant meatballs, always in a tomato sauce. Nick's freshly made pasta—his hazelnut-mushroom lasagna, or the cheese ravioli—enlivened our sensibilities with their extraordinary flavors. Nick's was on the cutting edge of a gourmet trend, and we had the good fortune to ride the wave with him. What synchronicity that the rise of fresh gourmet food and wine intertwined as Nick's and the Oregon wine industry gained fame together.

One night we made what turned out to be an irrevocable decision—we took the kids with us to Nick's. They had been begging for some time. Nik was fourteen, Alex was eleven, and Alison was five. They were on their best behavior all evening. Alison, when she got so tired and full she couldn't stay awake, quietly climbed down and lay under the table like a sleepy puppy. Bill and I looked at each other across the table and knew we had come to the end of an era.

☙

By the mid 1980s, the family tensions, especially with my brother Ronnie, had stretched to the breaking point. The Sokol brothers had started looking at their investment as essentially subsidizing Bill and me. It's hard to tell who was more motivated—they to get their money out or Bill and I to have them out of our business.

But finding a nonfamily investor was neither easy nor appealing. We longed to own it all ourselves. We tried different proposals to my brothers, one of which involved trading my future inheritance for their shares in the winery, but my potential inheritance was not enough to cover the value of their shares. However, it was enough to cover their ownership of the vineyard, which was a separate company. So I traded my portion of my parents' estate for my brothers' portion of the vineyard. We were finally sole owners of at least part of our business.

We didn't bother to look for entrepreneurs to invest in the winery. We knew they would lose interest fast when they saw the numbers. Wineries have never been moneymaking investments. For entrepreneurs, owning a winery would be a lifestyle investment made after they had accumulated a bundle and wanted to surround themselves with some of the finer things in life. Owning a winery in Oregon, in those years, was not glamorous enough to qualify.

But there were other reasons for people to invest. We had been buying grapes from two vineyards, both owned by friends. Neither of them wanted to start a winery, and ownership in Sokol Blosser would ensure a home for their grapes. We were thrilled at the prospect of dealing with friends as partners and having a stable supply of local grapes. We broached the idea to them, they were interested, and the sale went through in 1987. The family tensions slowly began to ease. By the time we gathered for my father's funeral in March 1988, relations were guardedly cordial between Bill and my brothers.

Our new partners were Hyland Vineyards, about twenty minutes away toward the coast, and Durant Vineyards, which was contiguous to our land. Hyland was owned by four couples, the Kreimeyers, Welches, Markleys, and Trenhailes, and managed by Jack Trenhaile; Durant Vineyards was owned and run by Ken and Penny Durant. Bill and Ken were longtime friends; both had worked at the same engineering-planning company. We enthusiastically welcomed our new partners, who together owned 50 percent of the winery. The twelve of us spent hours brainstorming ideas and making optimistic plans. Bill and I went to California with Ken Durant, Vic Kreimeyer, and Jack Trenhaile to visit tasting rooms in Napa and Sonoma and get ideas.

One of the highlights of the trip was a visit Bill had arranged with Tim Mondavi to the Robert Mondavi Winery. After touring the production area, Tim showed us into a private room where a special tasting with Mondavi's senior enologists had been set up for us. Entering the room, with its white tablecloths and rows of glasses and wines at each place, and realizing that this had been done for us, impressed us greatly. We decided to do the same for special guests at Sokol Blosser from then on. Three Mondavi senior enologists, Ken Shyvers, Russ Rosner, and Charles Thomas, led the tasting. We enjoyed the VIP treatment.

We returned to Sokol Blosser full of ideas, hopeful about the future, and highly motivated to get going on our plans. We built a new, two-story addition to the winery—a private room for tastings and meetings on the first floor and an office above. Bill had been working out of a cubicle in the tasting room, so the new office, even with its used furniture and industrial carpet, was a welcome relief.

We also decided it was time for a new winemaker. This was a difficult undertaking, since there was not a big pool of expertise in Oregon. Bill talked to Russ Rosner at Mondavi about working for us, but at that time Mondavi was a winemaker's dream and leaving California for the hinterland of Oregon had no allure. When we decided to promote our cellarmaster to the position of winemaker, Russ agreed to consult for us and provide a safety net. Our plan was that Russ would visit Sokol Blosser to taste and help with blending, and to give advice on our barrel program and other winery practices. Between his visits, our cellarmaster-turned-wine-maker would stay in contact with him by telephone. The Robert Mondavi Winery was doing a lot of innovative experimentation, and we hoped to benefit through Russ. Russ visited Sokol Blosser four times and consulted with us for two years, but our winemaker wanted to do things his own way. He never telephoned Russ without being prodded by Bill, who was so preoccupied with running the other parts of the business that he didn't push it.

⁙

By the end of the 1980s, an active and growing wine industry had been established in Oregon. The best restaurants in the state put Oregon wines front and center on their wine lists. California friends told me they had given up trying to sell their Pinot Noir in Oregon. While still fumbling for identity and recognition, Oregon wine was selling coast-to-coast and start-ing to be sought after by wine buyers in prominent stores and restaurants. Vineyard acreage increased every year, and new wineries were dotting the hillsides. At Sokol Blosser, the orchards had all become vineyards, as had the old wheat fields across the canyon. Yamhill County continued to lead the state in wine-grape acreage and wineries, and auxiliary businesses had sprung up to service them.

A community of forty Trappist monks had moved from Our Lady of Guadalupe Abbey in Pecos, New Mexico, to Lafayette, Oregon, years ear-lier, locating less than five miles from the Sokol Blosser vineyards. They farmed four hundred of their thirteen hundred acres, made fruitcakes for sale, operated a bookbindery, and made church pews. The pew business dried up in the fallout from Vatican II, when Catholic church-building went the way of Gregorian chant, and the monks needed a new business for their empty carpentry shop. In the late 1980s, the abbey's business manager, Father Paschal Phillips, decided to see if Bill Blosser, Dick Erath, and a few other local wine people would welcome his idea of developing a bonded wine warehouse at the abbey.

Paschal was already one of my favorite people. I had met him when I was running for office. When the Catholic mayor of McMinnville, Ed Gormley, had advised me to go see Father Paschal, I'd been dubious. A monk? I should spend my valuable campaign time meeting a monk? Ed had smiled at me and said, "You'll see. Just do it." So I made an appointment and drove to the abbey to meet the man who was the monks' link to the outside world. The Trappists are a silent order; contemplation, not chitchat, was the rule. No radio or television, no newspapers or magazines. But they all voted, and at election time, Paschal educated them about the issues and candidates. I never knew for sure, but it certainly seemed as if Paschal had forty votes in his pocket.

Paschal was well-educated, quick-witted, charming, and full of ideas. He was always in the middle of several projects, with several more in the idea or planning stage. He was a human-rights activist, proposing legislation to protect battered women and lobbying for reverse mortgages for seniors. He completely shattered my monk stereotype of an otherworldly, retiring person who spent all his time in prayer. He had been a high-powered corporate attorney in Los Angeles and had left his high-rise, air-conditioned office for a cubicle in rural Yamhill County.

After my political campaigns, I still occasionally visited Paschal, or invited him to our home for dinner. I wasn't surprised when he came to see Bill with his latest idea. It was a departure from his humanitarian focus, but he was in charge of keeping the monks afloat financially, and the abbey needed to use its big empty space. He had tried renting it to private furniture firms, but none survived more than a few years. Paschal was looking for something more permanent and lucrative. With the increase in wineries and wine production in the area, his timing was right. The Trappists' new Abbey Wine Warehouse opened in 1990 with six wineries, including ours, storing 30,000 cases. We enjoyed telling people the monks were watching over our wine. The abbey's new venture became so much a part of the growing wine industry that the abbey started offering other services, such as labeling and shipping. It got so full it had to expand. A little more than a decade after its inception, the Abbey Wine Warehouse housed 280,000 cases of wine, from ninety-one wineries.

5

Turnover

The Christmas holidays of 1990 found us in Seaside, on the Oregon coast, in a large rented house with the extended family. We were ten—Bill's parents, his sister Taffy, his Aunt Dottie, my mother, Bill and I, and our three kids—plus Bagel. We bought the last tree in the local Christmas tree lot and decorated it with colorful paper cutouts. We played charades and Trivial Pursuit, ate fresh Dungeness crab, and shopped the post-Christmas sales. When we weren't with the family, Bill and I took Bagel and walked on the beach. We were in a serious, ongoing discussion about the winery and what we should do.

Bill had been running the winery full-time for ten years. The business was barely keeping up with its payables, and Bill was more discouraged than I had ever seen him. Sales were down. Funds were so tight that we hadn't hired any extra help for the 1990 harvest. Instead, we had cut back on production and used our administrative and sales staff to work the vintage. Bill's salary was about two-thirds of what he had been making before he came to the winery, and our standard of living had been slowly declining. We discussed our options.

Everything we had was tied up in our business, and we agreed that we needed to be less dependent on the winery. One of us could get another job, and I was the obvious choice. We tried to come up with something I could do. All we could think of was teaching. I had taught for a year at Beaverton High School, after I got my master's degree and before we went to Chapel Hill. I had been not much older than the seniors in my history and social-studies classes and was often mistaken in the hallway for one of the students. The principal who hired me, wanting some fresh ideas in the classroom, was then replaced by a man whose views were more traditional. Among the speakers I brought into my class was a friend who, talking about migrant workers, said "fuck." He was explaining that sex was a popular recreation, since it was free and migrant workers were poor. The principal, when he heard this, wanted to fire me on the spot. He couldn't, but he was clear about his decision not to renew my contract. "When I think of Susan Blosser," he said, "my ulcer acts up." I became a local cause célèbre with the then-nascent teacher's organization fighting to save my position. I savored the principal's quote as the only pleasurable part of an agonizing experience. Years later, after he retired, the principal turned up at the winery and asked to see me, as if we were old friends.

Bill pushed the teaching option until I admitted I really didn't want to go back to it. Besides, the issue was money, and the sad reality was that I had much less earning capacity in the real world than Bill. When we finally got everything on the table, we realized that Bill was feeling totally burned out with running the winery. On the other hand, I had become more and more interested in it over the years. The unexpected but suddenly logical conclusion was that I should take Bill's position as winery president and he should get a job in Portland.

The decision energized us both. Bill hadn't realized how much he wanted to get out, and I hadn't realized how eager I was to take his position. We worked out a strategy for presenting the news to our partners and employees. Part of our strategy was to redefine the president's job as half-time and propose that I be paid half of what Bill had been making. The money didn't matter; I wanted the opportunity. To this day, I'm not sure why the partners agreed. They knew how untested I was. I knew the grape business, and I had been involved in every aspect of the winery except winemaking. But I had no business training, no financial training, and no management training. The reality was that the winery couldn't afford anyone with more experience. They were willing to let me try, but on a tight leash.

There was no transition period. After we told the staff, Bill left and didn't reappear in the office. I had no job description to work from. I started by learning where everything was. The payoff was the freedom to do things my way. I rarely asked Bill for advice, and to his credit, he seldom gave it unless asked. The price I paid for that freedom was living in constant fear that I would make some stupid mistake and reveal to everyone how little I really knew about what I was doing.

From the moment I took the president's chair, I saw problems that needed immediate attention in every part of the operation. They reminded me of the boulders that bubbled up in the vineyard soil and had to be moved to prevent equipment problems, but worked well for landscaping elsewhere. That tired cliché, "Turn lemons into lemonade," was my mantra as I confronted operational boulders and looked for ways to make them work for us.

The partnership with our vineyard-owner friends, which had started with such promise in 1987, began to disintegrate after several years. We should have foreseen it—our interests were not aligned. Hyland Vineyards and Durant Vineyards had become winery owners to assure a home for their grapes and to return money to their vineyards. As 50 percent owners, they had the right to provide 50 percent of the grapes for each harvest, and to take part in setting the price for those grapes. That price could be, and often was, higher than the general market. The winery had to take their grapes, regardless of whether they were the best grapes available or there was sufficient market for wines they made. The agreement meant that we made the wine we had grapes for, not necessarily the wine that would sell best. In other words, it made us production-driven, not market-driven. I learned how exactly backward that was.

For two years we sent profits back to the vineyards through an elaborate bottle-pricing formula, but then we had years without profits. Our outside accountant made us realize that we had given away our profits in the good years but weren't getting comparable concessions from the vineyards in the bad years. The tough years without profit fueled conflict among us, as, I am sure, did lack of faith in my management. By late 1991, Hyland was looking for someone to buy its shares, and my relations with the Durant and Hyland owners could best be described as civilized but hostile. I know that Bill, commuting to Portland, was glad to be removed from the turmoil.

By then Alex and Alison were riding to Portland with Bill to attend a private school, so Bill suggested we move to the city. I could commute to the vineyard. When Bill first floated this idea, I was horrified at the thought of moving away from the vineyard, even though it did make sense since three of the four of us still at home had to be in Portland all day. I was no longer working in the vineyard, and I did have meetings in Portland more and more; it was a logical move. I was reluctant, but once we were settled in the heart of downtown Portland I quickly realized the advantages. Two blocks from Nordstrom's and near our favorite downtown restaurants, our apartment overlooked the city's park blocks, which were full of big old trees, grass, and flowerbeds. We got used to hearing sirens and street sweepers at night instead of coyotes and crickets. I didn't even mind the forty-five-minute commute. In many ways, it was a relief to get physically away from work.

During this difficult time, while I was learning to manage the winery and the estate vineyards, cope with poor sales and excess inventory, refinance debt, and deal with the supplier-owner problem, I relied on our outside accountant, Jack Irvine, to help me think things through. More than once, I called him in total frustration, angry with myself for not knowing what to do. He kept telling me to think of how the pearl in an oyster grows—by friction against a grain of sand within the shell. He told me to think of myself as the potential pearl and Hyland and Durant as the grains of sand, and that in years to come I would value that friction for the toughness it gave me. I sure needed that toughness, if only to cover my insecurity. I wished I could toss off numbers with the aplomb of an MBA, but my eyes glazed over discussing ratios. Whenever I was asked for a number, I had to look it up. At more than one board meeting I was close to tears as the partners treated my lack of financial savvy with sarcasm and disdain. Bill was present but silent at those meetings. I don't know what he could have said to help me, but I kept wishing he would come to my defense. I imagined myself donning a football helmet before board meetings, and I'd call Jack and tell him I needed my chinstrap tightened and a pep talk. Each meeting I was a little better prepared, but I felt alone and vulnerable.

While difficulties with our partners took up a good deal of emotional time, my daily priority was to motivate my staff, get sales moving, and generate some cash. I rented a house at the beach and took the five key people in production, sales, and accounting off for two days to plan our strategy. They had not understood how deep a financial hole we were in, and I could see both concern and determination on their faces when I asked them to help. Each contributed to the plan, and its impact was immediately apparent as employee morale lifted and cash from the sale of excess inventory started flowing in.

The second priority was to refinance the winery's debt. We were banking with a big Portland bank that we had selected in the mid 1980s partly because its president had called us at home to urge us personally to bank with him. Now, for reasons we could not understand, the bank was pressuring us to refinance elsewhere. We later understood that they were divesting themselves of small loans to position themselves for sale, but at the time we took it personally. While I looked for a new bank, Jack Irvine negotiated a substantial write-down of our existing loan to make us look more financially appealing. I contacted the banks that worked with other wineries, but I never got past the receptionist. When I mentioned our predicament to an old acquaintance, Andy Sichler, who headed the McMinnville branch of KeyBank, he agreed to talk. At that time, KeyBank had no wineries or vineyards in its loan portfolio—the field was considered too risky. I wrote up a very straightforward overview of the winery, explaining the difficult position we were in, the reasons for it, and my plan for climbing out. KeyBank agreed to refinance us. Andy told me later he never doubted I would do what I said. Andy and KeyBank took a chance and helped me when I needed it most, and I have been loyal to them ever since.

The next priority was national sales. While we had distributed nationally since 1981, three-fourths of our sales were still in Oregon, and we had been concentrating on moving wine wholesale through our distributor and retail in our tasting room. In August 1991, I terminated our contract with the national broker we had used since 1987 and decided to handle national sales myself, dealing directly with our distributors in the different markets. We were selling so little through our broker that I knew I could at least match his sales, and we would save the commission we were paying him. When I called each of the distributors, I was surprised and pleased to find that almost all of them welcomed me and wanted to continue doing business. Thus began my days of traveling, and of making lasting friendships in many of the markets.

While I had distribution in many good markets, our departed broker had left a big hole in New York City, traditionally the most important wine market in the country. I set out to find a distributor who would care about a little operation like Sokol Blosser. Friends pointed me in the direction of Lauber Imports, a smallish operation run by Ed Lauber and his son, Mark. I began the courtship process by telephoning Mark to chat about how we might work together. I sent wine samples, and then I flew to New York to meet with Mark and Ed. We hit it off, and in the late summer of 1991, Lauber Imports took on its first Oregon winery. Bill had flown to New York with me, and we spent that hot, humid weekend strolling in Central Park and eating at restaurants we hoped would soon sell our wine.

About that time, I took a hard look at myself in the mirror and decided that, as president of a winery with a national market, I needed to look more professional. The 1980s had been my Mother Earth phase—I plaited my long hair in French braids every morning, perfect for working in the vineyard. I had cut it short for my political campaigns and was now concerned about the encroaching gray. Other women advised me that while it was okay, even distinguished, for men to have gray hair, women with gray hair just looked old. I wanted glamorous, not matronly, so off I went to get my dark brown hair frosted. This led to my blonde phase. With each frosting, my hair got blonder and blonder, until finally I let go and went totally blonde.

Thirteen-year-old Alison suggested I engage a Nordstrom personal shopper to help me look presidential. She offered to come along and help. I sat in a large dressing room full of mirrors as the personal shopper swept in and out with different looks. I gamely tried the outfits on, discarding immediately the ones I thought either too trendy or too plain, lingering over others, trying to decide if they captured the stylish, professional look I was after. With Alison's approval, I came away with a new wardrobe, my favorites being a silver-gray silk pantsuit that flowed and draped elegantly and a pink wool blazer that seemed to brighten the world. I was ready to hit the road, meet wine buyers, schmooze with wine writers, and sell Sokol Blosser wine.

I soon learned that meeting the chefs, sommeliers, wine buyers, and wine media was just the beginning. They couldn't buy directly from me. I could get them interested, but the actual sale had to go through a distributor. So when I worked a market, I went with the distributor's sales representative (called a rep in the trade) to restaurants and shops, the best of which were besieged by distributor reps with their wine portfolios. If we were able to get the attention of the wine buyer, I talked about Sokol Blosser and the rep tried to make the sale. Often the account wouldn't make a buying decision on the spot and I would have to depend on the sales rep to follow up. The challenge was to get the sales rep to present my wine when I wasn't there. I essentially had to make two sales, one to the sales rep and one to the account.

Distributors make or break a winery's success in their market. Get two winery salespeople together and they will inevitably start discussing distributors' pros and cons. The distributors usually have a few effective sales reps and many who don't much care and will sell whatever is easiest, usually based on incentives, ratings, or cost. Big wineries offered perks like cell phones, TVs, gas barbecues, or trips to Europe or California or Australia as motivators. My goal was always to find and cultivate the few who would remember to talk about Sokol Blosser.

Of the many distributors I worked with over the years, I found only a few I respected and thought well-run. Measured against almost any standard, Lauber Imports landed at the top. Every April, Lauber hosted two "Grand Annual" tastings for the wine trade, a modest one in New Jersey and a huge one in New York, on the fourteenth floor of the glitzy Times Square Marriott Marquis. Owners, winemakers, and national sales managers flew in from all over the world for these events. We stood elbow to elbow at long tables for five hours, pouring wine for hundreds of wine buyers and wine writers. Behind us, at eye level, neon models sauntered across giant billboards advertising sportswear, martinis, and music.

*In Atlanta, doing an in-store tasting at Harry's Market (note the
totally blonde hair). I am standing in front of stacked cases
of the whole line of Sokol Blosser wine. That's as good as it gets.*

Jeanne Davis, from Turnbull Cellars in Napa, and I were among the regulars at the Lauber Grand Annual. We got into the habit of sharing a room to cut expenses and have time to catch up on each other's lives. In our free time, we walked and talked and shopped our way around Manhattan. One year we stayed at the Paramount, across from the Marriott Marquis. It was so hip it didn't have its name on the door. The lobby decor was in shades of black, and a single stainless-steel couch was apparently the only place to sit. Our double room was so small we had to turn sideways to get past the beds, and we were always tripping over our suitcases. Another year I arrived early evening, in a downpour, at the Marriott Marquis, looking forward to relaxing in our room, only to discover that there was no reservation in either of our names and no sign of Jeanne. I staved off the encroaching panic, found a pay phone (this was before cell phones), and called the winery, where, fortunately, Jeanne had left a message. She had procured a room in a hotel about four blocks away. Finding a cab seemed a bigger hassle than walking, even with the rain. I pulled up the collar on my coat, put my head down, and jostled up the street with the crowd, alternately pulling and pushing my heavy suitcase and trying in vain to avoid the puddles at the curbs. What a relief to see Jeanne at last and collapse in a room of our own.

Through Lauber, I made wine-industry friends from Argentina, France, Italy, California, and New York. Because we were together year after year, the wineries in the Lauber portfolio felt like an extended family. We looked forward to seeing one another at least once a year, and I always went out of my way, wherever I was, to order one of the Lauber family of wines in a restaurant; others told me they did the same. Only Lauber, among all the distributors I got to know, elicited a "family" feeling among the wineries in its portfolio.

Another happy consequence of my business relationship with Lauber

Imports was my friendship with Ed Lauber and his wife, Marsha Palanci. Through her public-relations business, Marsha became the source of many marketing adventures. I met some of my favorite people in the wine business through Ed and Marsha, who were well loved in the industry. I often stayed with them at their apartment on the Upper East Side. No matter the season or the weather, Ed's booming voice woke me in time for their six o'clock three-mile walk or run. Weekdays, we went along the East River and, on the way back, stopped for coffee and bagels at the corner coffee shop. Weekends, we'd walk through Central Park to a small pastry shop on the Upper West Side, near the cathedral of St. John the Divine. Ed and Marsha made New York my favorite market, and I tried to go there at least twice a year. Since I traveled by myself, it meant a lot to have friends, especially on weekends.

I also tried out large-scale events, such as the Aspen Food and Wine Festival, the Telluride Wine Festival, the Santa Fe Chile and Wine Festival, and the New Orleans Food and Wine Experience. Even with the added visibility of being on a workshop panel, my wine was lost in the sea of wineries. I was a regular at only a few events. For most of the 1990s, I participated in the annual Albany (New York) Wine Festival, held at the Desmond Hotel at the end of January. Ed Lauber usually drove me up, and I never left the hotel—usually because we were snowed in. Every year, before signing up, I questioned whether I was in my right mind, going to upstate New York in midwinter. One year, on my way to the festival, I met a woman from another Oregon winery in the airport and, of course, we asked each other where we were going. I said, "Albany, New York." She said, "Maui." I forced a smile, thinking, *What's wrong with this picture?*

From a business perspective, I actually looked forward to the Albany weekend. I could see all the upstate New York retailers and restaurant wine buyers who attended and, after the crush of customers during the tastings,

I could relax with the small group of regulars who came from other wineries. We compared notes on distributor difficulties, always a favorite topic, and shared industry gossip. More than once I heard news about my home turf in Oregon by traveling to New York. It was also my chance to keep up with the heart of the domestic wine industry, Napa and Sonoma, where most of the wineries attending were located.

Before or after Albany, I tried to include a stop at the Culinary Institute of America (CIA) in Hyde Park, New York, to teach a wine class, do a tasting for the students, and host a winery dinner for the public in one of the five student-run restaurants. I wanted that opportunity to talk about Oregon Pinot Noir in general, and Sokol Blosser in particular, to people I knew would someday be among the top chefs and restaurateurs of the nation. I always invited the students to visit Sokol Blosser and, over the years, a number appeared. From humble beginnings in a former monastery, the CIA had developed a campus full of corporate-named buildings and an applicant waiting list. In my business, *CIA* means chefs and gourmet cuisine, not undercover agents and nuclear bombs.

Based on the number of requests for donations I receive, I think every town, village, suburb, and city in the country has a wine auction for a good cause. There is only one outside of Oregon that I attended regularly——the High Museum Art and Wine Auction in Atlanta at the end of March. The weather was so unpredictable that one year I had to buy a winter coat to combat the snow flurries and another year I sweltered in 90-degree heat. But hot or cold, I wanted to be there because the auction and the events surrounding it were run so creatively, and it was clear that the organizers truly appreciated the attending wineries. Activities started two days before the live auction with a wine tasting that gave wineries the opportunity to meet Atlanta's restaurant and retail wine buyers. There were also dinners for art patrons in private homes, at which the wineries could display their wines to some of Atlanta's well-heeled consumers. But these were just the warm-up. The real festivities started with a black-tie gala on Friday evening, with a viewing of Saturday's auction items and a silent auction. The live-auction activities took place Saturday afternoon under the big top—a series of huge white tents, complete with flooring and chandeliers and decorated with colored lighting and extravagant floral displays. When I first heard the auction was to be in a tent, I was dubious, but this event redefined the word *tent* for me. Auction day started with two hours of wine and food tasting, with Atlanta's top restaurants participating. Just after noon, conversation was stopped by the arrival, seemingly out of nowhere, of the Marching Abominables, a zany band of thirty instrument-toting adults of all sizes and shapes, flamboyantly dressed in ruffled crinolines, spandex, and tie-dye. They sashayed around the tables and led the way into the auction tent, putting the crowd in just the right mood for an afternoon of intense bidding for art, lavish wine trips, and unique wine items. The auction raised big money for the High Museum.

Deciding what to contribute to this auction was always difficult. It had to be something really special. One year I had a local glass artist create a stained-glass lid for a large wooden box packed with six bottles of our best Pinot Noir. Other years I commissioned a replica of a traditional northwestern Native American bentwood box, with black and red animal totem figures silk-screened along the sides and ends—again packed with six bottles of our very best wine.

There was free time between wine tastings, and it was in Atlanta that wine friend Laurie Puzo taught me the art of "aerobic shopping." We whizzed through the sale racks in the stores at the Lennox Mall with the energy and speed of Olympic sprinters. It was a rare opportunity for me, and I went home with a bulging suitcase.

Our national sales grew steadily during the early 1990s, as Oregon wine became known and I spent more time on the road. I traveled as much as I felt I could and still run the winery. My rule of thumb was this: if I was traveling more than I wanted but less than I thought I should, I had reached the right equilibrium. Nik and Alex were off on their own. Alison was still at home, but she had started to distance herself from me—payback for my teenage years when I considered my parents a cross I had to bear. The mothers of her schoolmates were younger than I was and didn't work outside the home, so Alison saw me as embarrassingly different. She allowed me to pick her up after a school party, but I had to wait outside. We were oddly distant, yet close. I so badly wanted my daughter to have the relationship with me that I had never had with my mother, but during that time, I almost gave up. Then, when she was sixteen, she met Darko Spoljaric, the young man she would later marry. Darko convinced her to look at her mother not as a dingbat but as a woman running a successful business. She started to see me through different lenses, and we grew closer. During her senior year of high school, when she was studying in France and felt lonely, we wrote each other almost every day, via a brand-new medium of communication called e-mail.

Alison loved to travel, and I enjoyed taking her with me when I could. One summer while still in high school, she accompanied me to the Telluride Wine Festival. We spent time with other winery women, primarily two friends from Napa, Laurie Puzo from Domaine Chandon and Eugenia Keegan, president of Bouchaine. I admired and loved to be with those women. Experienced and well connected, they took me under their wing, introducing me to people they thought I should know. We gave one another the support and encouragement we needed in the male world of business. I wanted Alison to learn from successful professional women, and they generously mentored her. Eugenia even invited Alison to stay with her for a weekend in Napa.

Alison worked as my assistant one summer during college, and then after two years doing marketing and public relations at other companies, she came to help me at Sokol Blosser. We were just trying it out. One day she said to me, "Mom, I want to go back to school and get my MBA. I don't want to go to night school. I want to take two years off and go full-time. I'm going to apply to the University of Washington. Okay?"

I wanted to say, "Alison, don't go! I need you here." But, of course, I didn't. I sent her off with my blessing, hoping she would want to come back to the winery.

I knew Alison had seen the administrative side of the wine business. To give her a taste of the glamorous side, I invited her to go with me to the tenth anniversary of the High Museum auction in Atlanta. It coincided with her spring break at the University of Washington, and she was happy to put her books away, leave her little apartment, and come with me. The auction's theme was "Women of Wine," and I was one of ten women they were honoring. I had always attended the auction alone, so I was pleased to have Alison's company. On the first night, I took her to Canoe, a favorite restaurant where Kevin Good, the manager and wine buyer, was a friend. We had a fabulous five-course meal, sipping a different wine with each course. We relaxed and chatted with Kevin, and with Sonoma winemaker Merry Edwards and her husband, who were seated nearby, and ate until we couldn't fit in another bite. When I asked for the bill, Kevin said our dinner was his treat. What a grand, and rare, indulgence. Alison's eyes grew large, and I could see she was filing this away for reference as she contemplated the future.

National sales were our fastest-growing area, but we also had an active retail business at our winery tasting room, and we considered ways to increase the number of winery visitors. How could we entice them? Could we lure them out with music? I had envisioned music under the stars at Sokol Blosser since we started planning the winery, but the idea got buried over the years. I pictured a small orchestra playing Mozart while the audience sat on a grassy hillside, surrounded by vineyards, overlooking the valley. Concertgoers would spread red-checked tablecloths for their gourmet picnic dinners, open bottles of Sokol Blosser wine, enjoy the music floating across the lawn, and leave with good memories of the evening and the winery. My mother, who had grown up in Chicago in a musical family, had told me about summer concerts at Ravinia, in the early 1900s. The wealthy families would settle themselves on blankets while the servants took out candelabra for the family picnic. Servants were not in my picture, but affluent wine lovers eating, drinking, and listening to music certainly were.

My "music under the stars" dream resurfaced when a promoter who had produced successful soft-rock concerts at the Portland Zoo and other venues approached us. All we had to offer was space—a grassy area we could turn into an amphitheater. We had no stage, no electricity or water in the potential amphitheater area, and no good parking. And the county ordinance regulating large public gatherings was exceedingly stringent. Nicknamed the Woodstock ordinance, it had been passed to prevent the kind of festival that had gotten out of hand in Woodstock, New York, in the late 1960s. The ordinance had lain dormant on the books for almost twenty years, until we came along and called it into play. It required applying to the county for the desired date, detailing the purpose and the logistics, and then procuring the approval of the local fire department, the county sanitarian, and the county sheriff. Finally, with all these approvals in hand, I had to appear at a public hearing before the county commissioners. I'm sure the idea behind the ordinance was to make the process so cumbersome that no one would undertake it, and it had succeeded for many years.

I made an appointment to talk to the county commissioners informally, to gauge their response. I could see that the idea of bringing more visitors to Yamhill County appealed to them. Their main concerns were traffic flow and potential congestion on an already very busy state highway, 99W. We decided to apply.

We knew that Robert Mondavi and Wente in California and Chateau Ste. Michelle Winery in Washington had summer concerts of popular music, but no winery in Oregon had tried it. Gary Mortensen, my vice president, was a music buff and offered to take the lead in organizing it, so we dived in. For eight consecutive years, from 1992 until 1999, we had a summer music festival.

Reality forced me to give up the idea of Mozart, or anything classical, because it would not draw enough audience. We looked for popular performers who had big names but were no longer the hottest box-office draws, and thus were affordable. Harry Belafonte, Johnny Mathis, George Benson, Los Lobos, Tower of Power, Ray Charles, John Denver, the Neville Brothers, Little Feat, Joan Baez, the Manhattan Transfer, Al Jarreau, Tony Bennett, Nanci Griffith, Ricki Lee Jones, Steven Stills, and Peter, Paul and Mary all came to Dundee, Oregon, to perform at Sokol Blosser. Initially, we called the series Sokol Blosser Live. When I explained the concept to my friend Heidi Yorkshire, she slyly suggested we should have called it the Sokol Blosser—Are They Still Alive? concert series.

The first year, with the difficulties of applying to the county, setting up a stage, and booking performers, we produced only one concert. On September 18, an unusually warm, mellow night, Los Lobos performed before a sellout crowd. The audience sat on the grassy hillside eating dinners catered by McCormick & Schmick's, drinking Sokol Blosser wine, and swaying to the Latino beat. The evening was just as magical as I had imagined, only slightly marred by the parking-area congestion after the show.

The promoter came up with only two shows the second year, so we engaged a larger production company, and from then on we did five shows a season. The production company went to a lot of expense to expand the stage, set up the canopy and lighting, and bring in the amplification and sound system, so they wanted as many concerts as possible to recoup the costs. Because the concerts drained our staff time and energy, and I didn't want one every weekend, five was a compromise.

When we started the concerts, I hadn't thought it would be too big a drain on the staff. After all, the producer was taking care of production, traffic control, parking, and even the food vendor. Gary handled all the details with the producer and was the point person during concerts. My role at the performances was to be with our guests and to go on stage during intermission to welcome people, thank our sponsors, and honor the charity of the evening. But what happened when the food vendor was understaffed and people had to stand in line for an hour to get food? Or the performers took too long doing their sound check and people had to wait in the hot sun beyond the advertised entry time? Or there were long lines for the portable toilets? Or the traffic out of Portland was so bad that concertgoers arrived angry and late? Our staff had to deal with the many phone calls for information and the complaints. It became clear that people blamed Sokol Blosser for anything that went wrong, regardless of whether we were responsible. If the food wasn't excellent, or ran out, or was served too slowly, Sokol Blosser took the heat. I was a nervous wreck during the concerts, trying to watch the food line and security personnel and worrying about what could go wrong while smiling and trying to be a gracious host. I was at all thirty-six concerts over the eight years, and I don't even remember hearing the music at most of them.

Three concerts stand out in my mind—John Denver, Johnny Mathis, and Ray Charles—each for a different reason. John Denver's performance was one of his last, and the only one of our concerts that was signed as well as sung. During the entire performance, two signers at the side of the stage quietly alternated as he sang. They swayed silently to the music, their faces animated as they communicated with their hands. They were so compelling, the audience stopped focusing solely on John Denver, and the signers became part of the performance.

Johnny Mathis, who had been at the top of the charts when I entered high school, qualified for the "are they still alive?" comment. In the weeks before the concert, I was astonished by the number of phone calls from friends, and friends of friends, begging to meet him. No other performer had sparked this much interest. I was able to arrange what the producer called a meet-and-greet, so just before Mr. Mathis performed, I led a group of animated women, full of anticipation at meeting their idol, down behind the stage to his trailer. When we entered, he welcomed us, shook hands, and gave each woman a signed picture. I stood back, trying not to look as shocked as I felt. *Was this handsome man, radiating health and fitness, the same one I had listened to almost forty years earlier? How could he look so good?* There was a full moon that night, and as the mostly female audience sat on blankets and lawn chairs listening to Johnny Mathis croon "Chances Are," their dreamy smiles reflected their memories of romantic times.

On the other hand, I cringe and apologize when people tell me they attended the Ray Charles concert. We always monitored the weather, so we knew it was going to rain. We predicted attendance would be light. I should have known Oregonians don't stay home when it's wet; we had a full house as the rain settled in for the night. The only tented areas were for the concert sponsors, so most of the audience sat in the open amphitheater, under tarps and raincoats if they were lucky. Those without rain gear just sat in the rain. I couldn't believe so many people stayed. The electrical system shorted out during intermission, which delayed Ray Charles's appearance. And the wooden stage was too wet and slippery for much jiving.

When people tried to leave, they found our grassy gentle hillside parking area had turned to mud. Cars slid all over. Worst were the four-wheel-drive vehicles, because their owners assumed they could do anything. Alex ran down to the equipment shed to get the tractor and spent hours pulling cars over to the gravel driveway. His hands became so muddy and slippery that his five-month-old wedding ring slipped off. He never found it, though he combed the property on foot and with a metal detector.

Years later, a young woman named Brooke Anthony, who came to work in our accounting office, offered a more heartwarming view of the Ray Charles concert. She told me that she had been backstage with her mother and grandmother that evening, helping the local caterer feed the band. When the concert started, her grandma called her and her mother onto a wing of the stage. She remembered the three generations swaying to Ray Charles's beat and looking out through the dark rain at a sea of tarps also swaying back and forth.

For most of the 1990s, our summer concerts brought us cash and publicity. Then their success started to have a negative side. People would ask, "Aren't you the winery that does those great concerts?" I wanted to be known for great wine, not great concerts. Did we have to choose? It took a crisis to end the run.

In 1999, we decided to produce the concerts ourselves. We had watched three different production companies over the years, we knew what we had to do, and we thought we could do it better. The only danger was that we would be taking on the financial risk, which had previously been carried by the production companies. There was a surfeit of concerts that summer in Portland, and our lineup of performers wasn't strong enough to draw customers out of town. As a result, we never sold enough tickets. Our concert series lost so much money that I felt the winery was at risk. The combination of financial disaster and the toll on staff made me realize we couldn't continue. Concert fans were disappointed, but I was greatly relieved.

I made plans to plant most of the concert parking area. Our business was making wine, not music.

6

Vision

When I became president of the winery, my goals were to keep the business alive and get us out of a financial hole. I was so focused on generating cash, I didn't see what was happening in the wine world around me. Oregon's wine industry was evolving with new players. When I finally looked up, I saw that Sokol Blosser was being left behind. I spent several years trying to understand what was happening and then deciding what to do.

For the first fifteen years or so, there had been so few Oregon wineries that those of us with a national presence had the limelight. Then, as Oregon wines gained prestige, more and more vineyards and wineries appeared. The first international investment in Oregon was made in 1986 by an Australian winemaker and entrepreneur, Brian Croser. He created the Dundee Wine Company, which produced wine as Argyle Winery. Brian and his winemaker, Rollin Soles, planned to produce sparkling wine from the abundant Pinot Noir and Chardonnay in the area. Their first year, before their facility was ready, Rollin Soles made their wine at Sokol Blosser. Despite the fact that their winery was in a converted nut dryer right on Dundee's main drag, the Australian presence in Oregon did not make a big splash.

It took old-world investment for the wine world to sit up and take notice. In 1987, Robert Drouhin, the head of Maison Joseph Drouhin in Burgundy, bought a hundred acres close to Sokol Blosser in the Dundee

Hills. Robert's daughter, Véronique, had finished her enological studies in France and would be the winemaker—not moving to Oregon, but visiting at key times during the year to supervise the winemaking. Dave Adelsheim and David Lett had helped Robert find the site, and it was all kept very quiet until August 1987, when Governor Neil Goldschmidt made a public announcement.

Drouhin said, "There are only two places in the world I would plant Pinot Noir—Burgundy and Oregon." We were thrilled to have this kind of affirmation. After all, we had been there for seventeen years, saying the same thing. Our proclamations had fallen on skeptical ears, but when Robert Drouhin spoke with his money, people listened.

Robert started out buying grapes from local vineyards, including Sokol Blosser, and when he released his first wine, a 1988 Pinot Noir, he invited the local winegrowers to a reception in his cellar. He spoke about his new wine, saying that he was deliberately pricing it high to make a statement. Top Cabernet Sauvignon wines sold for fifty dollars or more, he said. Top Pinot Noir should be able to command thirty dollars a bottle. This was about twice as much as the rest of us sold our wine for, and we were both awed and thrilled. We all needed to make more money on our Pinot Noir, and if anyone could make it happen, it was Robert Drouhin. We cheered him loudly. "Go, Robert!" someone shouted.

Domaine Drouhin Oregon ushered in a slow but steady stream of new vineyards and wineries spilling all over the Willamette Valley in the 1990s. King Estate, WillaKenzie Estate, Archery Summit, Lemelson Vineyards, and Domaine Serene were all new operations that indicated significant investment—buildings that made architectural statements, the latest technology, extras like catering kitchens and beautiful landscaping, and winemakers with impressive credentials. Because the influx was a stream, not a flood, and because it was a while before each of the new properties had wine on the market, the results of all this new investment took time to manifest. The changes in the industry crept up on us. During the late 1970s and early 1980s, we knew all the newcomers. They came and talked to us and often worked a harvest at Sokol Blosser. Slowly, as the incoming stream grew, the personal contact lessened, and new names seemed to appear out of nowhere.

We had ringside seats watching Domaine Drouhin Oregon go up in 1988 and Archery Summit in 1992. All we had to do was look across our vineyard. We had such a good view that the owners of Archery Summit came to Sokol Blosser to observe the progress of their construction, and we got to know them. I suggested we install a coin-operated telescope aimed at these two wineries to take advantage of all the tourist interest. Early pictures of our vineyards show the wheat fields on which both of those wineries and their vineyards now sit. We blew up the pictures and put them, along with other old family pictures, in our tasting room. Sokol Blosser had history. Did anyone care besides us? The public was only mildly interested. The wine press and consumers were interested in what was new, not what was old.

Besides being one of the wine pioneers, what made Sokol Blosser special? Where was our niche? Our winery building, so modern in 1977, was out of date compared to the new wineries, which boasted gravity flow, the latest technology. And our John Storrs–designed tasting room looked small and shabby compared to the newer, larger, hipper places. We didn't have any foreign connections, like a French winemaker, owner, or investor. Once at the forefront of the Oregon wine industry, Sokol Blosser had slowed down and fallen into the middle of the pack. My radar picked up little of this at the time, though I watched as other older wineries, like Adelsheim Vineyard, took in investors and built beautiful new facilities. I was too busy getting Sokol Blosser out of its financial hole, producing concerts, and figuring out how to buy out Hyland and Durant.

For five years, we had sought resolution to the conflict with the two investor vineyards. We had tried to find other investors who would buy out Hyland and Durant's shares. We had looked at taking in additional investors. At one point, we had been so frustrated that we started to put together a deal to sell the whole winery. The influx of new wineries and vineyards had increased the demand for prime land and made our vineyards significantly more valuable.

Finally, it was the fact that Bill and I owned our vineyard separately from the winery that made resolution possible. Our vineyard had become worth enough that we could borrow against it to buy out Hyland and Durant. The possibility of total ownership of the winery made me giddy. I went straight to Andy Sichler at KeyBank, who had rescued us once before. The bank's appraisal of our vineyards indicated potentially sufficient value, depending on the price. Hyland and Durant were willing to talk about selling to us. Jack Irvine recommended John Hirschy, an attorney with experience in this realm, to help us. As I saw it could really happen, I stepped back to let Bill be our spokesman. Bill would have liked to avoid the risk that owning the entire winery entailed, so he was less eager than I. I saw our sole ownership as my salvation, and I wanted it so much I knew I would be a lousy negotiator. I stayed behind the scenes, whooping with joy whenever we reached a point of agreement.

The final transaction is etched on my brain. On October 26, 1996, at ten in the morning, Bill and I walked through the front door of a McMinnville title company and signed the legal papers that gave us full ownership of Sokol Blosser Winery. Twenty years after starting the winery with my father and brothers, we were finally able to claim it as ours alone. I felt an albatross drop from around my neck, even though the buyout took its toll on our balance sheet. From now on we would be accountable only to ourselves, and the destiny of the winery would be our choice.

Free to move forward, I looked around and began to realize how far behind we were. Sokol Blosser was producing about thirty thousand cases of wine annually. About half of it was "value-priced" Riesling, Pinot Noir, and Chardonnay that sold primarily in Oregon under our second label, SB Select. Sokol Blosser bottled twelve different wines, including four levels of Pinot Noir, three levels of Chardonnay, two levels of Riesling, a Müller-Thurgau, a Pinot Gris, and a rosé of Pinot Noir.

The second label had been a two-edged sword. By providing cash flow during tough times, it had kept us in business and provided a way to use our partners' grapes. On the other hand, our presence in the market with an inexpensive line devalued our image as a high-end winery. Distributors found it easier to sell the inexpensive wine and ignored the higher end, so as second-tier sales increased, sales of our higher-end wines slowed. Which path did we want to follow?

I wanted to grow excellent, flavorful grapes and create top-quality wine, not simply move *x* number of boxes, so for me the decision to compete on quality, rather than price and volume, was simple. Implementing it was not, and I spent the next year grappling with the right vision for Sokol Blosser.

It was not as easy as eliminating the SB Select label. If we got rid of the second label, how would we generate cash flow to take its place? When we were no longer beholden to our partners, whose grapes did we want? We still had land to plant; was it time to reevaluate what we should be growing? If we decided to do anything different, how would we manage the transition? After the huge loan to buy out our partners, could we afford more debt to do anything else? The right path was not clear to me, and I spent a lot of time looking at financial projections and talking with Jack Irvine and with Eugenia Keegan, my good friend who was by then president of Vine Cliff Winery.

Cosmetic changes were easier, and I knew we needed a new look. Our wine-label design was twenty years old. What once had seemed elegant now appeared stodgy. Gary Mortensen, our vice president, suggested Sandstrom Design as the most creative in Portland, and the firm fulfilled our expectations. Sally Morrow, the designer who worked with us, gave us just the look we were after—stylish without being stiff, simple without being plain. The label debuted in the summer of 1997 and won immediate praise from both consumers and the wine industry.

To get publicity and national visibility for our new label, I hired Marsha Palanci in New York. Marsha came up with the perfect plan. Television stations shied away from promoting wine directly on their local morning talk shows, but cooking segments were the rage, sandwiched between weather and traffic updates. If I could give a cooking demonstration, it would be natural to pair a Sokol Blosser wine with the dish. Marsha could place my cooking segments in every market I visited. It was genius—free publicity and lots of visibility for Sokol Blosser, everywhere in the United States.

Marsha knew I had studied teaching and was relatively at ease speaking to groups, but suggested a quick course in media training to hone my TV presentation skills. She picked Lou Ekus, whose office was a two-hundred-year-old converted gristmill in western Massachusetts, and whose client list included such luminaries as cookbook author Lynne Rossetto Kasper and chef Emeril Lagasse. Marsha talked me into it, reassuring me she would go along for support. I decided it might be interesting, and I would at least learn something. We began by choosing recipes to demo that would go with my wine. The first inkling that Marsha's grand plan might not work was when I realized I had no repertoire of recipes from which to choose. I never had time to cook, but I owned some wonderful cookbooks. Ignoring my doubts, I consulted a cookbook by Marie Simmons, a friend Marsha had introduced me to, chose several recipes I thought looked good, and tried them out.

The cold, rainy February day matched my dour mood as Marsha and I flew to Hartford, Connecticut, rented a car, and made our way along the back roads of western Massachusetts to Lou's house. The two-day training involved videotaping me in Lou's demonstration kitchen, with him acting as host; watching and critiquing the tape; and then doing it all again. And again. And again. The goal was for me to be able to teach the recipe and create the dish in the time allotted, usually about six minutes, while maintaining friendly banter with the host. It was like that old game of trying to rub your head while patting your stomach.

I had suspected that the process would be painfully embarrassing. And it was, though I did learn a lot. I learned not to "up talk," that is, raise my voice at the end of a sentence—a common female foible. I learned how to reduce my overall message to a few key points and then "bridge" from whatever question the host asked back to those points. I learned to connect with the audience through the host, who was the reason they were watching the show. And I learned how important it was to be high-energy exaggerated by a factor of two, to compensate for the deadening medium of television.

By the end of the two days I was able to make the recipes, smile, and talk at the same time. Lou gave me a video of my final performance. I had spent a lot of money on this piece of education. Was I ready to start a media tour?

I went back to the winery and immediately got embroiled in day-to-day business, pushing all thoughts of a media tour to the back burner. But the experience was gnawing at me, and it soon occurred to me that Marsha's ingenious plan had a fatal flaw—me. I couldn't in good conscience put myself in the public eye as an accomplished cook. I have friends who are passionate about cooking, who whip up intricate dishes with ease and competence, or who cook as a way to relax. I don't fall into any of those categories. I am more likely to be the person they cook for. I love gourmet food, but I have neither the patience nor the desire to be a chef. My cooking demos would be a sham. Shamefaced at my culinary inadequacy, I told Marsha I couldn't do it. The video from my media training sits untouched on a shelf. I've never had the courage to watch it.

Meanwhile, we were finishing another of Marsha's inspirations, one that I wholeheartedly endorsed—Sokol Blosser's competition to define the character of Oregon Pinot Noir. "If Pinot Noir were a person, who would it be? Choose a famous person, living or dead, who you think best personifies Oregon Pinot Noir. Write a short essay describing your nominee. . . ."

That was our challenge. The project was another public-relations dream because it had so many opportunities for media attention. Marsha put out a press release to the wine media to announce the contest, and then six months later another one to announce the winner, followed by a big press luncheon in Manhattan.

A wide variety of people, both male and female, were nominated. Words like *charming, sophisticated, elegant, graceful,* and *subtle* kept reappearing in the essays. But the differences were what made it interesting. Colette was nominated for her sensuality, evocative quality, and tendency to be a tease; Maya Angelou because she was poetic, intense, lively, complex, and visionary. Two first ladies, Jacqueline Kennedy Onassis and Hillary Rodham Clinton, were candidates. Two actresses, Katharine Hepburn and Catherine Deneuve, were cited for their beauty, elegance, and complexity. The male entries ran the gamut from Lee Iacocca, for his ability to take a difficult situation and make it golden; to Fred Astaire, for his sophistication and ability to dance across the floor like Pinot Noir across the palate; to David Bowie, for his otherworldly transcendence and nonconformity; to Clint Eastwood, for his multifaceted talent. None of these nominees won.

I had asked two friends with impeccable credentials to be the judges:

Steven Koblik, wine lover and erudite president of Reed College, and Heidi Yorkshire, author and wine columnist for Portland's *Oregonian*. They unanimously chose the entry proposing Cary Grant as the epitome of Pinot Noir. The winner, Steve Heimoff, wrote that Cary Grant best characterized Oregon Pinot Noir because "his personality was romantic, urbane, charming, seductive, sophisticated. He had lots of style and finesse. He possessed youthful charm, yet he aged well. He was graceful, elegant, and debonair. His voice and mannerisms were silky smooth. His style was seamless. All the parts came together in harmony." He may have been describing Cary Grant, but this is also the best-ever description of Pinot Noir.

I sent each person who entered the contest a bottle of Sokol Blosser Pinot Noir with a note thanking them for participating. Steve spent a week in Oregon wine country as our guest, including attendance at the International Pinot Noir Celebration in McMinnville. The media lunch Marsha arranged at a restaurant in Manhattan was so well attended that we were squeezed into the room. Guests were welcomed by a huge poster board of Cary Grant looking his most elegant and seductive and received a gift video of his movie *To Catch a Thief*. I loved everything about this project.

One of the best parts of working with Marsha was meeting her friends, other professional women connected to wine and food. They were mainly writers, but in different arenas—some specialized in cookbooks, others wrote only for wine publications, still others wrote for lifestyle media. Most lived and worked in New York or California. It felt good to be around other professional women in related fields, and our animated discussions, always over food, ranged from analysis of Martha Stewart's popularity to meal descriptions and anecdotes from recent tours to Tuscany or Sicily or Greece.

I had two gift tickets, round-trip between New York and Portland, that had to be used, so I asked Marsha if we could bring wine writers to Sokol Blosser. She made arrangements with two of her friends from New York,

Nancy Wolfson and Marguerite Thomas, to come to Portland one June weekend. I had never met either woman, but I knew Nancy had been beauty editor at several women's magazines, including *Glamour,* and Marguerite was a published author who wrote regularly for wine magazines. I waited eagerly at the airport gate, especially curious to see what a beauty editor would look like. I was watching so carefully for two women with extensive makeup and expensive clothes that I hardly glanced at the two simply dressed women who walked over to me and introduced themselves. Nancy and Marguerite weren't that different from me. I relaxed immediately, and it felt even easier when I learned they hadn't met before they got on the airplane. By the end of the visit, the three of us felt like sisters and have been friends ever since. As their recreation director, I not only showed them around the winery; we took a guided tour of Portland's Japanese Garden, went kayaking on the Willamette River, attended a baroque chamber-music concert in one of Portland's historic churches, and ate at as many Portland restaurants as we could fit in. We spent the last afternoon at my home in Portland, and while they walked down Northwest Twenty-Third Street to see the shops, I collapsed on the couch, exhausted.

Kept busy by all the public-relations efforts and the daily push to sell our wine, I was still struggling to find the right identity for the winery. What did I really want? I couldn't force a vision, so I could only hope my subconscious was working on it while I kept the business running. I guess it was, because as the new year of 1998 began, the fog started to lift.

It was January, and I was in New York City. After a hectic morning calling on accounts, one of the Lauber sales reps and I were relaxing over lunch. I sensed he had something on his mind. He finally worked up his nerve to tell me that he was concerned about Sokol Blosser's wine quality. He was blunt. Lauber Imports had just taken on Domaine Drouhin Oregon, right up the hill from us. His comments went like this: Sokol Blosser was located close to Domaine Drouhin, right? So the grapes from the two vineyards would be comparable, right? Then why wasn't our wine from recent vintages as good as theirs? In other words, did we have a winemaking problem? He looked at me anxiously, afraid he had overstepped his bounds. I looked back silently, not because I was insulted but because a light bulb had just gone off in my head. I realized he had just articulated something that had been simmering gently in the back of my brain for some time. We did have a great vineyard site. Why hadn't this translated into superlative wine quality? I remembered that one of the first questions Eugenia had asked me when I said I was ready to go after high quality was whether I had the right winemaker to take me there. I had equivocated at the time, and she hadn't pressed, but now I wondered if she had been trying to get me to face the situation.

I am not, and never wanted to be, a winemaker. The vineyard and the business captured my imagination; I wanted to put winemaking into the hands of someone I trusted. I am awed by the way a great winemaker combines art and science—most people's talents lie in one territory or the other. A winemaker uses chemistry and microbiology as the foundation for intuitive judgment. Like a great chef, the winemaker goes beyond the recipe, beyond technique, into the realm of creativity, using informed intuition to make crucial judgments at each step. But there's a fundamental difference: a chef can re-create that great dish night after night. A winemaker can make wine only once a year, when the grapes come in. And if the wine must age, it may take years to find out whether it is fabulous. There will be only about thirty vintages, or winemaking opportunities, in a winemaker's entire career. A profession in which the outcomes are so few, and each is so vital, requires tremendous patience, focus, skill, and passion.

In our segment of the market, there is no substitute for wine quality. Neither excellent marketing, nor management, nor sales personnel can compensate for lack of flavor in the bottle. This makes the position of wine-maker arguably the most important position at a winery, and the most difficult to fill well.

I had made my decision; I needed a new winemaker before the next harvest. I knew I faced a daunting task. There were no Oregon winemakers I wanted to pursue, but a California winemaker would be more expensive, and would be used to different grapes and a different wine lifestyle. How was I going to find someone I could afford, who understood Oregon Pinot Noir? I called Eugenia in Napa to see if she knew of any assistant winemakers who might be willing to move to Oregon for the challenge of making great Pinot Noir. I was disappointed when she called back to tell me she'd struck out. Suddenly I thought of the Mondavi enologist who had helped us years ago.

"I want someone just like Russ Rosner," I told Eugenia. "He has it all. He is familiar with Sokol Blosser, he understands Oregon fruit, and he has top-notch training." Eugenia knew him slightly and agreed. I knew he had worked at an Oregon winery for a while, but neither of us knew what he was doing now. Eugenia picked up her local phone book, and there he was. She offered to call Russ and test his interest, and asked whether she should reveal my name. I told her to go ahead. I wasn't sure whether knowing it was Sokol Blosser would make him more or less interested, but I thought we might as well find out.

"You'll never guess what Russ is doing," Eugenia teased when she called back.

"What?" I could feel my pulse quickening.

"Nothing!" she almost shouted. "He isn't working, and it sounds like he's trying to decide what direction to go."

"Is he interested in Sokol Blosser?" By now my pulse was racing.

"Yes," she said.

I took a deep breath and let it out slowly.

I flew to Napa, filled with hope and trepidation, and interviewed Russ over the next two days. Bill flew down for the second interview. Russ was the same serious guy I remembered. Work and fly-fishing were his passions. No family or entangling relationships. He had lived in Napa, the center of quality winemaking in the United States, for the past sixteen years. Moving to Oregon was a step he would consider, but not take lightly. He had several other job options at larger operations, but I could see that working with Oregon Pinot Noir, and being the only winemaker, appealed to him. There was so much to do at the winery; I didn't want someone whose decisions and behavior I had to monitor. I wanted someone with the skills to do the job and the integrity to do it honestly and responsibly, and I was willing to give that person significant control over the whole production realm. Was Russ Rosner the right one? And if he were, how could we convince him to come work for us?

Bill and I agreed, as did Eugenia, who sat in on the interviews at her house, that Russ could be the right person for Sokol Blosser. He wasn't flashy or even outgoing, but solid, dependable, well-trained, and passionate about wine quality. If anything, we worried that he was too serious, too detail-oriented. Eugenia called some people who had worked with him, and when her report came in favorable, we sent Russ a proposal and offered to fly him up to see the facility. He declined to visit, and then deliberated for three weeks, apparently struggling with the decision to leave Napa. I was getting increasingly nervous, knowing I had no backup plan. Finally, he called. Yes, he would start in July and move to Oregon in August. It would be a huge change for Russ and for Sokol Blosser. I fervently hoped it would work.

That spring I also thought long and hard about whether I really wanted to bring any of the kids into the business, and whether I should. I had urged them all in other directions, but Alex kept circling back. Years before, I had hired him to work in the cellar, but our partners had objected strenuously when they found out, arguing that it was too awkward for the winemaker to supervise an owner. I was furious and embarrassed; I had to go back and tell Alex he couldn't work for us. His response was to go across the hill and take a position as vineyard foreman at Archery Summit, which was just planting its vineyards. From there he had gone back to college to finish his bachelor's degree, and he was now working for a wine wholesaler in Portland.

I needed to hire someone to help with sales, and Alex had the qualities I was looking for. No more partners, so the decision path was open. Alex wasn't pushing to come into the business, but his warmth and interest in others had made him good with people from the time he could talk. I thought about how, as a small boy, he had engaged others in conversation. "Grandma, how was your day?" he would ask, reversing the typical adult-child exchange.

But I knew bringing Alex into the business was more emotionally loaded than just hiring a new employee. How would this affect our relationship? How would the other employees react? Would I be too soft with him—or too hard? What if it didn't work out? Everyone knows stories about family businesses in which siblings and parents end up mired in anger and hostility.

On the other hand, why shouldn't I be mentoring my son in the wine business? Wasn't that one of the benefits of a family business? What could be better than working with someone you love? My friend Jackie Gango, a successful art-gallery owner, had both her daughters working with her; the business was flourishing, and she loved the arrangement. After agonizing for months, I went ahead, spurred on by the need for help in the national market and my joy at the thought of working with one of my children.

Russ and Alex both started in July. The little guy who used to stand on a chair to do the dishes now had a desk near mine.

"Mom," he said on his first day, "what should I call you at work?"

"Susan," I replied. "We need to be businesslike."

We managed to keep up the formality for a while, but gradually defaulted. At a fancy wine dinner, or when he was standing in front of a distributor's sales force trying to get attention for Sokol Blosser, Alex's references to "Mom" only reminded people that we were truly a family business.

⁘

Russ and Alex arrived on the scene as we debuted Evolution No. 9, a brand-new product that we had created to solve an old problem. We had been producing Müller-Thurgau wine since the first vintage, 1977, but it had always been borderline for profitability. In the fall of 1997, Alan Dreeben, head of Block Distributing in San Antonio, started me thinking when he suggested, semiseriously, that I come up with a proprietary name for our Müller-Thurgau. The wine was good, but its odd varietal name made it hard for his salespeople to sell.

I'd never considered that, but why not? My Müller-Thurgau, retailing at $7.95, was so low-margin that it was good only for absorbing overhead. I had to do something that would make it more profitable. Would a proprietary name do the job? I didn't think so. How about making it a blended wine? Most white blends retailed for no more than ten dollars, but I did know of one that was well-regarded and sold for a good price. It was called Conundrum, was made by a California winery, and retailed for about twenty dollars a bottle. It became our model. When I took the idea back to Gary, he was ready to start working on it right away.

First, we had to find a name and create the package. Credit for the clever, offbeat name and label goes to the design team of David Brooks and Sally Morrow. Their genius was in creating something that was original and imaginative without crossing the line into cute, corny, or trendy. Sally had designed our new Sokol Blosser label the year before. David, a close friend of Gary's, had written copy for our brochures, ads, and invitations for years, and had declared himself the keeper of our image. But they had never worked together for us, and it became a magical collaboration.

A casual remark by a wine friend shaped a key part of the program. Joshua Wesson had sold many cases of Müller-Thurgau for us in his Best Cellars store in Manhattan. We met for coffee in the early spring of 1998, when I was in New York for Lauber's Grand Annual tastings. By that time, we had the concept of the blended white wine and the name Evolution No. 9. I wanted Josh's reaction, and maybe even his blessing and encouragement. I admired his wacky sense of humor, way with words, and keen business sense, and I was not alone; he had a large following. He lamented the passing of Müller-Thurgau as an individual wine, since he had been so successful with it at his store. But he liked our new project and, almost in passing, said, "I assume by the name that the wine will be a blend of nine different grape varieties."

I hadn't linked the name with the grapes, and nine varieties seemed like a lot. "Do you think that's important?" I asked.

"I think it's critical," he said.

Bingo! The decision to make the wine a blend of nine varieties, made that morning over coffee on the Upper East Side, became a keystone of the marketing program. We had been planning to blend only three or four white varieties, but it turned out to be easy to come up with nine. In the showcase vineyard right outside our tasting room, which had started out as a test plot of different grape varieties for an Oregon State University research project, we had rows of Muscat, Müller-Thurgau, Sylvaner, Pinot Blanc, Gewürztraminer, Chardonnay, Riesling, and Pinot Gris. With the addition of Sémillon, we had our nine varieties.

My Texas broker at the time suggested that we highlight the new wine's affinity for what he called "cuisines of heat." Müller-Thurgau went so well with spicy foods, the new wine should, too. Restaurants were moving to lighter menus, with recipes that contained complex flavors of cilantro, mint, lemongrass, ginger, cumin, hot chiles, or wasabi. These flavors did not match well with heavily oaked Chardonnays and tannin-laden Cabernet Sauvignons, but Evolution No. 9 complemented them beautifully.

When the wine came onto the market, in the early summer of 1998, our distributors were dubious. This wine was unlike anything they had seen, and they weren't sure the public would respond. The label had an attitude, with its big "No. 9" on the front, and there was a little booklet dangling from a key chain on the neck of the bottle. One of our best distributors, in Northern California, told me he didn't think it would sell because it wasn't serious enough. It's true that we wanted the packaging to be the antithesis of the traditionally snobby wine label and deliberately chose not to put either a vintage date or an appellation on the label. But the wine itself we took very seriously.

Some understood the label immediately. Liner & Elsen, a wine store in Portland run by Bob Liner and Matt Elsen, wrote it up in their monthly newsletter, saying,

The "hottest" new white wine from the Oregon wine country doesn't come from some new trendy startup winery. It's not made by some visiting celebrity French winemaker either. It's not a slick marketing trick conjured up by some transplanted Californian who flew up here from Chateau Bigbucks in Snapanoma. No, the wine that's all the rage is "Evolution No. 9"—it's the tastiest new wine on the shelf and it comes from none other than the winery at the top of the long and winding road, the venerable Sokol Blosser Winery. The packaging is terrific, and the wine. . . . well, "Nothing like it has ever been." 9 varietals come together. Pour it backwards and walk across the street barefoot. Drink some. Huge, tropical fruit bouquet (the Walrus was Paul), off-dry, lush, koo-koo ka-choo, crisp finish. May it serve you well. Yeah, yeah, yeah. . . .

We read that write-up in awe. They got it.

Our California distributor watched as opinion leaders in the Bay Area embraced Evolution No. 9. Leaders in the gay and lesbian community in San Francisco bought it enthusiastically, partly because Vivien Gay, a friend of ours and a leader in that community, talked it up. But there's also no substitute for luck, and that came when Gene Burns, a radio personality whose Saturday morning program on San Francisco's KGO had a huge audience, invited me to be on his show. He had tasted our new wine at a local restaurant, on the recommendation of the waiter, and had loved it so much that he wanted me to talk about it on his program. If I had ever had any doubts about the power of the media, they were erased by the deluge of inquiries and sales after Gene's show. Not only were Bay Area stores bought out of Evolution No. 9, but the winery had to keep one person on the phone all that day, taking orders.

Evolution No. 9 was a bold new concept for us and, in fact, for Oregon. It started slowly, but when it found its niche in the market, sales rose steadily. Production started in 1998 at 2,700 cases and increased twelve-fold in five years. Conceived as the solution to an ongoing problem, it became a home run in its own right. The combination of an engaging name, an ingenious label, and great flavor made it a winner in every sense. How did we get so lucky? We didn't do any of the things big corporations do in developing new products, mainly because we didn't have the money. Sokol Blosser's research-and-development department consisted of Gary, my vice president, and me. How happy, how serendipitous, how desperately needed was this success.

⁘

Earlier that spring, I had been asked by a prominent Portland retailer, Made in Oregon, with whom we had long done business, to be part of its new advertising campaign. The company wanted to show the public that real people, not faceless corporations, made the products it sold. Its ad, scheduled to appear on billboards all over the city, would feature three of its suppliers. Already lined up were a salmon fisherman, who would hold up a shimmering fish, and a woodworker, who would hold a polished myrtle wood bowl. Made in Oregon asked me to be the third, holding a bottle of our wine. I suspected that I was the token woman, but I didn't care; I was thrilled at the free advertising for the winery. We were photographed separately and the art director composed the final image, so I never met the two men. Nor did I see the ad until it appeared three months later, larger than life and in living color, in the seasonal catalog and on posters at the Portland airport.

I forgot to tell any of my kids. In July, I got a phone message from Nik. "Hello, Mom? I was just driving on I-5 into Portland and there you were,

*Larger than life, looming above the freeway, I smile down
from the "Made in Oregon" billboard. (Photo by Rizzo Studios.)*

looking down at me from this giant billboard. I almost drove off the road.
What's going on?"

I called back and left him a message in my sternest, most authoritative
voice: "Nik, you never know where I'm going to be. Mama is always watching you. Don't you forget it!"

When my three brothers came to visit our mother that summer, I
couldn't resist showing them how important their little sister was. I made
sure that, as we drove around Portland, we passed one of the billboards.
Made in Oregon was so pleased with the promotion, the company kept it
going months longer than first planned; I smiled at motorists from those
billboards for more than four months. To capture this for posterity, just

before the promotion ended and the billboards came down I asked my photographer friend, John Rizzo, to photograph them all for me.

⋮

By October 1998, Evolution had been endorsed by enough opinion leaders to get attention in the marketplace, Russ was successfully weathering his first vintage, and Alex was learning the business. The business side of my life was taking on a healthy glow. But I could no longer ignore how unhappy my personal life was.

Judging from appearances, our marriage was a success. Sure, we had had our troubles, but we had built a business together and had three great kids. The difficulties were on the inside. During the hectic years of building the business and raising a family, we had suppressed our personal needs. It was all family and winery, winery and family. Once, in August 1993, I had left, so frustrated with Bill that I never wanted to speak to him again. My friend Karen Hinsdale, on whose doorstep I landed, advised me not to stop talking to him, no matter how mad I was. It was difficult for me to stay civil, but it was good advice. When I calmed down, I did miss him. Joint counseling brought us back together. Over the next five years, we saw our kids go off to school, get married, and launch themselves into orbits of their own. Then it was just the two of us. I wasn't angry anymore, but I had begun to feel trapped. Something important was missing.

Once again, Eugenia helped me. She drove from Napa to join me at the end of my October sales trip in San Francisco, and we stayed up late talking. She had a new love, someone I knew, and she was telling me about their relationship. When she emphasized how nurturing and caring he was, tears started flowing down my cheeks. I was thrilled for my friend, but these were not tears of happiness. I had realized while she was talking what was wrong. It was that nurturing I craved, and I had never had it. Not from my parents. Not from Bill.

One of the psychologists I went to told me I was a "pleaser," and I could see what he meant. I spent my childhood and my marriage trying to please my parents and my husband, always thinking that for them to love me, I had to make them happy. My mother undoubtedly didn't realize that when she said, "Susie, you're such a good girl. I love you," I would conclude that the latter depended on the former. But I did. In the hope of praise, acceptance, love, I hid my own feelings. As I focused on pleasing everyone, my emotional life became so confused that I lost track of what I really wanted. The sad part is that trying to please didn't work. I always felt that nothing I did was ever quite enough.

Being the decision maker, first at the vineyard and then at the winery, forced me to identify what I wanted on a business level. After I learned to do that, I felt like two people. At work, I was at ease, competent, and decisive. I liked that person. My success running the winery gave me confidence I had never had before, and I relished the feeling that I had done something competently. At home, I was still a pleaser, submerging my feelings to be the person I thought Bill wanted. As that person, I was easily depressed. Despite the many winery crises, I laughed and smiled more at work than I did at home. I didn't want to be two different people; I needed to put the pieces together. I didn't think it was possible within the context of our marriage.

In the late fall and winter of 1998, our relationship unraveled despite frank conversation and many visits to a counselor. When I had tried to separate myself before, I had been angry and feeling the victim. Now I realized I was also the perpetrator. I had put myself in the position of pleaser. While Bill had allowed and even encouraged that role, I could have upgraded our relationship significantly if I had stood up to him by being true to myself, instead of being the person I thought he wanted me to be. Now Bill was willing to try, but I wasn't. We had too much negative history. Marriage had started to feel like a cage. I needed to be alone, to feel free. I was fifty-four years old and knew that I would probably never find anyone else—men my age wanted someone younger. I would most likely be alone for the rest of my life. That was tough to accept, but when being alone began to seem preferable to staying married, the decision was made.

I moved out in the waning days of December, filled with fear at being on my own and sadness at admitting failure after so many years. But deep inside, a small spark of anticipation flickered. With the exception of our nine-month separation, I had never lived alone: I had gone directly from my parents' home into marriage right after college. I found a little apartment overlooking the park blocks in downtown Portland, where YumYum and I set up housekeeping. I deliberately left with little more than my clothes, a few books, and my two treasures—the samovar my great-grandmother had brought with her from Russia in the 1880s and a large wooden loon carved by Amanda Crow, a present from my brother Ronnie. I wanted a fresh start.

What a difficult and melancholy job, to try to turn my back on almost thirty-three years of marriage. I was afraid I would wake up one day and realize I'd made a terrible mistake. Each morning I gingerly probed my emotional state to reassure myself that I was still okay with my decision. The kids were shocked. Since they were all married, with homes of their own, I thought they would take it in stride. That was a major miscalculation. They knew Bill and I had gone through tough times in the past, but since neither of us had confided our personal problems to them, my leaving caught them by surprise. They took our stability for granted, and losing it exploded their view of reality. I could feel their sympathy, but also

VISION

their distress that I had broken up the family. I wanted to explain how I felt, but I was uncomfortable talking to them about my relationship with their father and ended up with generalizations that were unsatisfying. Their chagrin didn't change my mind, but did show me how tied together we all were, and how my leaving Bill, while it satisfied my need, sowed chaos in the family. I had to defend an act so purely selfish.

My mother chastised me when I called to tell her the news. She was such an independent person herself, I thought she would congratulate me, but she clearly thought I had made a mistake. Nobody would invite me to parties, she said. Single women are like fifth wheels. Being invited to parties was so far from my line of thought that I didn't know how to respond. When I didn't get the sympathy I had hoped for, I stopped talking to her, causing friction on that front. I had finally done something the way I wanted, rather than trying to please others, and I was taking a lot of heat for it. Avoiding my kids and my mother, to escape the tensions, isolated me. I was glad to go to work, where I knew people would be friendly.

I was hesitant and awkward when I told people that Bill and I were no longer together. Business associates always asked how Bill was. If I said we had separated, everyone immediately assumed that Bill had left me and said how sorry they were. That facile assumption annoyed me, but blurting out that I had left him didn't seem right either. It took me over two years to be able to tell people matter-of-factly and not be embarrassed. I was brought up to believe that divorce was failure, but I have seen the more recent concept, the "good divorce," and I think that describes Bill and me. It was so civilized. When the air cleared and we realized that this time it was final, we acknowledged to each other that we had done a good job of raising the kids and building a business, but had not been successful with each other personally. But we also knew that we shared bonds neither of us would ever have with anyone else, and that we would always be joined on some

level. We went to the courthouse together to file for divorce, so that neither of us would have to suffer the indignity of being subpoenaed.

What made sense for me emotionally took a heavy toll financially. Oregon is a community-property state, so everything is considered to be owned
fifty-fifty in a divorce, regardless of how it has been owned before. This
was a blow; my status as majority owner of both the vineyards and the winery vanished with divorce. I had come to identify with the winery and had
put so much energy and emotion into it; I wanted to own it all. I found
that I would have to trade virtually everything else just to get back a majority share. It was a simple decision; I still had work to do to move the winery forward, and I wanted the control to be able to do it. Bill was willing
to let me buy him out, and it took us about two weeks to agree on the dis-
position of our interests. We turned it over to the attorneys—his, mine,
and the winery's—who then took almost eighteen months to work out
the details and get it in writing.

I was exhilarated by the thought of owning the winery myself. But as
time passed I mellowed, and I began to see that while buying Bill out might
have satisfied me emotionally, it was not the best strategy for the business.
Bill's experience was valuable and he would be helpful in mentoring our
children. Alex had come up with a plan in which he, Nik, and Alison would
defer income from their share of the vineyard to create retirement income
for Bill and me. The money was the same for Bill whether he stayed in or
got out, and when he decided to stay in, I took it as an affirmation. I found
myself glad to keep Bill involved.

While Bill and I were breaking up, I welcomed the challenges at work that
kept my mind off my personal troubles. There was always something. Unex-

pectedly, we were threatened with a lawsuit over Evolution No. 9. The phone call came the morning of December 7, 1998. The man at the other end identified himself as Alan Newman, president of Magic Hat Brewing Company in Vermont. He got right to the point. Someone had showed him our Evolution No. 9 wine bottle, and he thought we had a trademark infringement with his #9 Ale. Magic Hat had a trademark on "#9," and he thought our wine looked close enough to cause confusion in the consumer's mind. He called me to talk before going to his attorney. I had no idea how serious this was, but the words *trademark infringement* and *lawsuit* made my stomach convulse. Only one thing mitigated my displeasure at this bomb dropping out of nowhere on the anniversary of Pearl Harbor: I was fascinated by the uncanny coincidence that our two little companies, at opposite ends of the country and with similar products, had come up with the same idea at the same time.

That phone call from Alan was the beginning of several months of negotiations between us, without attorneys, and we became friends. Before accepting that I would really have to change our wine label, and maybe the name, I tried to talk him into joint marketing, asking him to picture stacks of our Evolution No. 9 wine next to stacks of his #9 Ale in stores around the country. We could do joint tastings and dinners. He listened, even sounded intrigued; but his board was adamant. We joked that one of us should buy the other out, each of us suggesting that the other should do it. But in the end, the only thing that would make him happy was for us to remove the big number 9 from our label. We finally hammered out an agreement that we both felt good about, partly because we each got something we wanted and partly because we did it ourselves. I agreed to cease sales of Evolution No. 9 in his top markets in New England and to take the big 9 off the front label. He agreed to give me nine months to use up the labels I had, which gave us time to have put two vintages of Evolution No. 9 on the market before we needed to modify the label. That would give us enough time to get it established, and the label could then "evolve."

Negotiating without attorneys was, I am convinced, the reason we accomplished so much so quickly. I had a lot of legal advice, as I'm sure did Alan, but all behind the scenes, only to keep me from getting into more trouble. Attorneys I consulted were eager to go to court, certain that Sokol Blosser had an excellent chance of winning. I resisted; I didn't want the emotional or financial drain of a lawsuit.

We asked Sally Morrow and David Brooks to "evolve" the label and the name, and they more than met the challenge. They came up with the "Chill. Pour. Sip. Chill" slogan, which we trademarked along with the shortened name, "Evolution." The transition to the new package was seamless, but the original name seemed engraved in people's minds. I still see Evolution listed on wine lists or in reviews as Evolution No. 9. Sales continued to grow exponentially, a wonderful phenomenon that provided the cash flow we needed to revitalize Sokol Blosser.

⁙

If I had any illusions about a new winemaker being all we needed to achieve higher quality, they were quickly dispelled. I started to see our production facility through Russ's eyes. I knew our old winery building and equipment hadn't kept up, but now I saw that it was more than just old; it was an impediment to making great wine. Russ admitted that if he had accepted our invitation to visit and seen how inadequate our facilities were, he probably wouldn't have taken the job. Russ pushed us to define our commitment to quality. People talk glibly about quality, he said, but few realize how much focus and commitment it takes. If high quality was our vision, how far were we willing, and able, to go to achieve it?

*Russ Rosner became winemaker at Sokol Blosser in 1998
and led the drive toward higher quality. (Photo by Doreen L. Wynja.)*

It was a hard question. We had to take a serious, strategic look at every part of the operation, not just winemaking. It took me two years to come to terms with what we needed to do. Then I had to find a way to implement it. We looked first at the production side, for the things that were easiest to agree on and put in place.

Russ recommended keeping our Pinot Noir in barrel more than twelve months, perhaps sixteen or eighteen months, before bottling. We had always bottled before harvest to be able to use the barrels for the upcoming vintage. If we kept the wine from the 1998 vintage in barrel through the 1999 harvest, we couldn't make as much wine; we didn't have enough room to keep two harvests in barrel at the same time. We decided to cut our Pinot Noir production in half to improve quality, and to buy a higher percentage of new French oak barrels each year, retiring the oldest barrels. To increase production, we would need a bigger cellar. We also lacked temperature and humidity control for our barrels; our winery, though built into the hillside, was not insulated. It was always too cold in winter and too hot in summer. We weren't ready to tackle a new building. We shifted our attention to equipment.

Our whole crush setup was antiquated. The crusher-stemmer and press beat and battered the grapes. New technology emphasized gentle handling, so we bought a new destemmer and a new press that met this criterion. Gravity flow, the concept of gently moving grapes or wine by gravity rather than by pumping, was not even in our vocabulary when we started making wine in 1977. By the 1990s, it was the buzzword. Starting with Domaine Drouhin, new wineries highlighted gravity flow in all their marketing literature. Short of building a new facility, what could we do? Russ came up with a way to simulate gravity flow where he felt it was most important, during the initial crush process, from sorting the grapes to transferring the crushed pulp and juice to the fermenter. The conveyor system would need to be custom-built. From friends in Napa we learned that the best conveyor systems were made in Newberg, Oregon, less than seven miles away. They had originally been designed to serve local cherry and nut growers.

The conveyor belt allowed us, for the first time, to look at each cluster and sort out any that didn't look ripe and healthy. The white grapes went directly into the press as whole clusters, another first for us. Whole-cluster pressing resulted in greater purity of fruit, less bitterness from the skins, and overall higher-quality wine. But it also made the pressing process slower and more cumbersome, since the press could hold only half as many grapes. For Russ's first vintage at Sokol Blosser, he put eighty-six tons of white grapes through our old, small press, two tons at a time, so the white wines could be done whole-cluster. His commitment to quality evinced a standard new to our cellar.

The Pinot Noir was destemmed directly into small fermenters, another quality change. This eliminated pumping the fruit and made it a gravity-flow process. The new equipment was all in place for the harvest of 1999, just in time for the vintage that I have come to consider one of the best in Oregon's short history, even better than that of 1985.

We had made a good start in our commitment to quality, but we also had to consider the ramifications for sales and marketing. There were further difficult decisions to be made about narrowing down our line of wines, upgrading our image and reputation, creating the right ambience in the tasting room, and what personnel we needed to carry out all our plans. There was a lot of work ahead, but after years of floundering, the vision was taking shape. I knew where I wanted to take the winery and felt focused and energized.

I look back on 1998 as a time of tumult and upheaval on all fronts, business and personal. Over the course of twelve months, I hired a new wine-maker, brought my son into the business, launched a new wine, and left my husband of thirty-three years. I had started to discover myself, the person underneath the "pleaser." It was no coincidence that this was also the year I stopped dyeing my hair blonde and let it return to its natural color, by then mostly gray.

7

Renaissance

That one year, 1998, created enough momentum to keep change in the air for the next five years. And when the dust finally settled, we were a winery with a new look and renewed purpose. Pursuing my new vision, I became so immersed in business that I gave up everything else. In the early years of my presidency, Bill and I had taken vacations to the Caribbean, Tuscany, Mexico City. One year I had gone with female friends to a spa in Mexico; another year we had rented a hillside villa in Puerto Vallarta. I had traveled to the annual meetings of the International Women's Forum and devoted significant time to civic boards and committees. But once I'd set my goals for revitalizing Sokol Blosser, I didn't want any distractions. My business consumed all available time and energy.

We now had a new winemaker, whose dedication to quality bordered on obsession, and new equipment in time for the 1999 vintage—a conveyor belt for sorting the grapes, a gravity-flow system into the press and fermenters, and a new press that gave us whole-cluster pressing capability. I turned next to the vineyards, a subject Alex had been pushing.

We had land we could plant. We had an open seventeen-acre parcel that we had been leasing to a local farmer since we'd pulled out the orchards; too many acres of Chardonnay; and a block of grapes, the Goosepen Riesling, that had succumbed to phylloxera.

Phylloxera. It had been years since I had given it much thought. Before we put a vine in the ground in the 1970s, we had known about this almost microscopic root louse that feeds on the roots of vinifera vines. The scourge of the industry, it had decimated the vineyards of France in the nineteenth century and threatened California in the twentieth. The most successful way to deal with it was to plant vinifera vines on resistant rootstock, bred from native American grape varieties. Our early research taught us that phylloxera existed in southern Oregon. Along with the other early growers, we debated about whether to go ahead and plant our vines directly into the soil or to graft them onto rootstock. Rootstock would affect the vine's growth habits, and no rootstocks were being used in Oregon in the early 1970s. We suspected that what worked in California wouldn't work for us, since everything else we did had to be modified because of the different growing conditions. In the end, we all took a calculated risk and planted our vines on their own roots, without rootstock, knowing that the phylloxera would eventually find us and hoping it would take a long time. Then I forgot about it as more immediate challenges captured our attention. We were lucky for eighteen years.

In August 1990, phylloxera burst on the scene and terrorized the Oregon wine industry. It was detected when Oregon State University (OSU) horticulturalists Bernadine Strik and Steve Price were called to a vineyard to discover why some vines were dying. About two hundred vines formed the classic circle, or lens, that is typical of phylloxera damage: the insects start on one vine and then spread out in concentric circles. The OSU scientists dug up roots of the affected vines and saw the phylloxera. Before that week was over, we had received a letter from OSU announcing that phylloxera had been found in the Dundee Hills and urging everyone to look closely at their vineyards for possible infestation. The letter did not name the vineyard, and, of course, this caused alarm and considerable speculation about who it might be. It turned out that the first vineyard to identify phylloxera damage was Gary Fuqua's old vineyard, planted about the same time as ours and only a few miles away. The second vineyard to find phylloxera was Sokol Blosser. We, who prided ourselves on being the first in so many wine industry achievements, were chagrined at being ahead of the curve in this disastrous one. But like our more positive firsts, we were not in the lead for long. When Bernadine and Steve started looking for it, phylloxera cropped up everywhere. Within two years there were more than thirty sites identified in the Willamette Valley. After a few more years OSU stopped counting and assumed it was everywhere in the soil.

The whole Oregon wine industry panicked when the news got out. It was the vineyard version of AIDS, and people reacted with the same mixture of fear, apprehension, and confusion as in the early AIDS years. *"Did you hear about . . . ?"* People whispered the word *phylloxera*. Growers wanted to know how to prevent contamination. Wineries wondered what to tell the media. No one knew how to handle the situation.

Bernadine Strik, OSU's extension viticulture specialist, the first to identify the phylloxera, took a leadership role in calming the alarmed growers and fearful wineries. There was basic research to be done. How phylloxera spread and at what rate it would spread in Oregon were still unknowns. Meanwhile, winegrowers felt they had to do something, and vineyard owners started requiring visitors to wear special booties when entering their vineyards or to walk through boot dips that would kill the phylloxera. Moving equipment or grape totes between vineyards suddenly held the prospect of spreading phylloxera, and the practice was discontinued or the equipment thoroughly washed between vineyards. The names of the vineyards where phylloxera had been identified were held closely within the industry. Vineyard and winery owners' first concern was to make sure their operations weren't contaminated; their second was to protect the industry as a whole from negative public relations.

As one of the first vineyards to be identified as having phylloxera, we found ourselves at the center of the maelstrom of alarm and confusion. We located a circular pattern of weak vines in the middle of our Goosepen Riesling and called Bernadine and Steve out for a look. They brought their shovels, and we trooped out into the vineyard to dig up roots close to the vines. I looked on as they made the positive identification and was able to see the tiny yellow gelatinous beasties myself, clinging to the roots. How could this little creature upend a whole industry? My brain swam with the possible implications of having a vineyard infected by phylloxera. I was baffled by how the phylloxera had made their way to our vineyard. I had no idea how to prevent its spread or what I should do about our affected block of Riesling. I didn't even know if the grapes from affected vines were safe to use in our wine. Maybe I should just rip out the whole block. I looked to Bernadine for advice and appreciated her calm handling of the situation.

In September, Bernadine and Steve wrote a special report called the "Phylloxera Issue," which the Wine Advisory Board sent to all wineries and vineyards, laying out the situation. While we were one of the two vineyards that had positively identified phylloxera, neither was mentioned by name. Probably this was done to protect our privacy, but the secrecy had the effect of making us feel tainted.

The life cycle of this little root louse became a hot topic of conversation among growers. We learned it had multiple generations throughout the summer and fall and that late summer to early fall was the time of highest populations and therefore the most important time to prevent contamination by equipment or by soil on boots. We started farming the infected Goosepen Riesling block in isolation—spraying it separately and washing the tires and equipment well before going into another block. We did hand-work or picked that block at the end of the day so that workers wouldn't go from it into another block with the insects on their boots. We did all this knowing that the phylloxera was probably everywhere and we were only slowing down its spread with these measures.

The rootstock trials that OSU had been conducting took on increased importance, and information about the results of these was disseminated. Domaine Drouhin had used phylloxera-resistant rootstock when it planted in the late 1980s, and we and other Willamette Valley growers looked to their practical experience with the new rootstocks. In addition to the steps taken to inform the industry, an aerial photography program to map the rate of spread was started, and Bernadine guided her students' research to further knowledge about how phylloxera operated in Oregon conditions. One student, Anne Connelly, in doing research for her master's thesis, found that phylloxera produced only two to three generations per year in Oregon, compared to as many as five in California. But the new information came in slowly, and for several years after the first phylloxera were discovered, panic and confusion were the norm.

We debated about how the phylloxera got to us and concluded that it came on grape totes from Fuqua's vineyard in the 1980s when we had bought grapes from him. It had developed slowly because we had permanent cover crop in that block and didn't stir up the soil, which would have promoted its spread. The Fuqua vineyard block had been pulled out and replanted immediately, but I continued farming our Riesling for six more years, finally pulling it out when the phylloxera's reach had made the block no longer economically viable. The Goosepen Riesling vines were twenty-four years old when we pulled them out.

I'd put off planting our available land because of the expense, but Alex convinced me we were sitting on a prime vineyard site and needed to use it. We could grow all the Pinot Noir we needed. A newspaper article by an Associated Press writer had called Dundee the "epicenter of the Oregon wine industry." If the highest and best use of our hillsides was Pinot

Noir, we had better grow more of that and less Chardonnay. If we replanted, we could try some of the new Burgundian Pinot Noir clones (numbers 115, 667, and 777) that had received rave reviews and use a closer spacing. I wasn't sure what that spacing would be, since we were seeing new plantings in the region with spacing varying from three by three feet to six by ten feet, our old standard. Everyone we asked had a well-reasoned argument for what he had chosen to do.

We had planted our vineyards somewhat haphazardly—whenever we bought more land, we had planted Chardonnay, Pinot Noir, and Riesling, with the result that we had small blocks of these varieties dotting the hillside. If we replanted, we could lay out a master plan and take advantage of what we had learned about the microclimates on our hillsides. Fully planting our vineyard would also give us control over more of the fruit for our wines, and we would be less dependent on growers, who were often difficult to deal with. My old friend Andy Sichler at KeyBank came up with an innovative financing solution: the bank would approve up to twelve thousand dollars an acre to establish vineyards, written like a construction loan— we could take out money as needed and pay only interest during the establishment phase. In the fourth year, when the grapes came into production, we would amortize the loan and start paying it off. We were the first ones to take advantage of this new KeyBank program. We ordered enough plants for thirty-two acres. They would be ready to plant in the spring of 2000.

New ideas were in the air during the 1990s, which gave me support for the way I wanted to do business and dramatically changed the way I farmed the vineyard. I had grown up thinking the world of business was Machiavellian—do whatever it takes to succeed. My idea of the corporate

tycoon was modeled on the nineteenth-century robber barons I had studied in American history—pillage the land, take advantage of the workers to build your fortune, and then give a little back so you can go down
in history as a great philanthropist. When I took over the winery, I didn't
want to play that way. I tried to keep my head down and quietly move my
business forward. Then, in the early 1990s, Len Bergstein, whom I had
known from my political career, asked if I would be interested in joining
with other like-minded Portland businesses to start an Oregon chapter of
Business for Social Responsibility (BSR). The national BSR organization,
just gaining ground, had been founded by well-respected companies
including Stride-Rite, the Gap, Levi Strauss, and Ben & Jerry's. It emphasized concern for people and the environment as well as for profit—the
"triple bottom line." When I heard that phrase, *triple bottom line,* for the
first time, I was thrilled: a pathway to reconcile my personal ethics with
the business world did exist. Our Portland group was composed of small,
lower-profile operations, but I remember well how relieved I was to find
values-driven cohorts in the business world. I was the only winery person, and I enjoyed my new friends in different fields.

In addition to being on the policy-making board of directors of the new
organization, a few of us met monthly just to talk about our companies.
We called our diverse, informal group "Business with Soul." Once the organization was up and running, the founders slowly drifted off to effect change
in other arenas. With its emphasis on values, BSR laid the foundation for
my later work with sustainability, giving me the courage to do what I thought
was right, not just what I thought would be profitable.

Shortly after my experience with BSR, my approach to farming changed
in a way that was so fundamental and so significant that it affected my whole
worldview. My outlook had changed gradually, my awareness slowly deep-
ening. When I read Wendell Berry's *The Gift of Good Land* and Michael Pol-

lan's *Second Nature* and *The Botany of Desire,* something clicked in my psyche. I felt, more deeply than ever, the interdependence of all living things, the perilous consequences of chemical agriculture, and how doomed we will be if we don't start repairing what we have done to the earth. What took me so long to get to this state of understanding? There is truth in the saying "When the student is ready, the teacher will come."

When we started the vineyard in the 1970s, we farmed like the other grape growers and local farmers, using chemicals to combat pests and disease, and synthetic fertilizer to make the vines grow. Using synthetic chemicals was the norm. We considered ourselves environmentalists, so we used the chemicals sparingly, but we accepted that they were necessary. When we sprayed diazinon or malathion to get rid of the cherry fruit fly, we were thinking only about our crop, not about the ecosystem. Chemicals were an immediate fix for pressing problems. Our friend and neighbor Ted Wirfs hated that his chemical arsenal had been compromised when arsenic sprays and DDT were banned in the 1950s. "Haven't had a good crop of peaches since," he would lament. Ted considered himself a good farmer and believed he was taking care of his land. Using chemicals to keep crops clean, the reasoning went, was part of being a good farmer.

No one considered that the chemicals killed more than just the pests they were aimed at. But in fact, many killed everything they touched. Conventional farming considered the soil a growing medium, so if chemicals killed the microbial life and made it unable to nourish plants, the solution was to replenish with synthetic fertilizer. The human mind is adept at embracing opposing beliefs without seeing a conflict. Farmers who considered themselves "stewards of the land" saw no problem in using toxic chemicals that sterilized the soil and damaged the ecosystem.

The underlying assumption was that the farmer's job was to tame, or at least control, nature. But making farming a battle for control assures that the winner is never going to be the farmer. Nature always wins; it's just a matter of time. Chemicals that worked well when they were introduced have proved to be temporary fixes; the pests they aimed to control developed resistance. As smart as we humans think we are, the "lesser" forms of life—weeds and insects—outsmart us every time. We have, however, succeeded in destroying groundwater, stream, and river quality and endangering the health of many species, including ourselves, by saturating the ground and air with chemicals that have penetrated every part of the food chain. As a result, we are ingesting high levels of synthetic chemicals through the air we breathe, the water we drink, and the food we eat.

Health problems have reached such proportions that ordinary citizens are demanding change. Concerned people have looked back to old-time practices and begun heeding the small voices of organic and biodynamic farmers. A "radical" new concept emerged: work with nature, rather than try to control it. Recognize the dynamic interrelationship of all living things. Everyone has some level of understanding of this interrelationship, even if it is only that we are all God's creatures. But most people don't realize how deeply it pervades every part of our lives or see people's role within it as cooperative rather than dominant.

Working with nature means building up the soil to be able to provide nutrition to plants naturally, instead of chemically—like the difference between normal digestion and intravenous feeding. Working with nature means encouraging a diverse array of species to establish an ecosystem. Instead of using chemicals to eliminate bugs and disease, we need to create a competitive environment in which no bug or disease can dominate. This approach, called sustainable agriculture, or agroecology, allows farmers and environmentalists to be on the same side.

A gentle push toward sustainable farming came from a new program developed by the Pacific Rivers Council, headquartered in Portland. The group created a Salmon-Safe designation to bestow on farms that produced their crops without harming salmon. This environmental marketing program was developed with the belief that if people knew and had a choice, they would choose products that helped protect salmon. In the vineyard, it meant limiting toxic chemicals and preventing erosion and runoff that could clog streams and rivers. The Pacific Rivers Council announced the Salmon-Safe program in the spring of 1996 at a press conference with TV coverage at Sokol Blosser. The task of educating the public began that day with the news media, who were full of questions about how farming on our hillsides and protecting salmon were related.

The following year, Ted Casteel from Bethel Heights Vineyard and Al MacDonald from Seven Springs Vineyard formalized a sustainability program imported from Europe that they called LIVE (Low Input Viticulture & Enology). Oregon's LIVE program was one of many sustainable programs in the United States, but was the only one with international recognition through the International Office of Biological Control, a prestigious European certifier. The program encouraged farmers to see the vineyard as a whole system, established guidelines for sustainable vineyard practices, and offered ecological options that encouraged biodiversity and reduced use of synthetic inputs. This way of looking at farming was so different from what the growers were used to, it took time to grasp. But when growers understood that vineyards would be healthier and longer-lived, they signed on, and the LIVE program garnered enough support to become institutionalized in Oregon. Salmon-Safe and LIVE later worked together on certification. After a three-year transition period, the first vineyards earned LIVE certification in 1999. Sokol Blosser was among that group. Once a review panel ensured that the wines weren't flawed, wineries could display the LIVE symbol on their label. Bethel Heights was the first winery to do this. The problem was that no one understood what LIVE meant.

Marketing sustainability was not yet in vogue, and I didn't believe that the Salmon-Safe or LIVE designations would really help us market wines unless we supported them with mega advertising and promotion, for which none of us had the dollars. What interested me more was finding out how sustainability really played out on the ground, in my own vineyard. Once I understood the importance of LIVE's central concept, biodiversity, I looked for ways to implement it at Sokol Blosser. Since we grew only one crop, wine grapes, we needed to take elaborate measures to create enough biodiversity to provide the necessary competition. A monoculture is an open invitation to predators of that one crop.

In my cover-crop experiments in the 1980s, I had searched for a single species that would do the job. Now I saw the value of planting a combination of species that would do triple duty by increasing microbial life in the soil, attracting beneficial insects with their flowers, and adding organic matter to the soil. To enhance the soil ecosystem, called the soil foodweb, I wanted compost—rich, sweet-smelling, and full of earthworms and microbial life. First I bought it, and then we started making it ourselves, using our own grape pomace (the grape stems and skins left after pressing), horse and cow manure, and straw. We let the cover-crop mixes we planted in the fall grow high in the spring before we mowed and worked them in to build up the humus content of the soil.

The large trees on the perimeter of our vineyard, which I'd seen before only as roosts for grape-eating birds, I now saw as wildlife habitat for the hawks, owls, raccoons, deer, and coyotes that were important players in our vineyard ecosystem. We joined the Prescott Western Bluebird Recovery Project and put up nesting boxes sized for the bluebirds. They and the swallows formed our insect patrol. In a few years, we had a small flock of bluebirds that were monitored and banded each season by volunteers. Driving up the winery road every morning, we would see them sitting on vine-

We built this compost pile by layering cow manure, straw, grape pomace, and rock phosphate. Thick flakes of straw protected the finished pile, which was about a hundred feet long and six feet high. This picture was taken on a cold morning, and you can see the steam rising from the pile. We wanted the pile to generate a heat of 130 degrees Fahrenheit to kill disease organisms. (Photo by Doreen L. Wynja.)

yard wires, and the flash of brilliant blue was always a thrill. When I helped with the banding, the baby bluebird whose tiny body pulsated in my hand symbolized the miracle of all the diverse life in our vineyard ecosystem.

Growing up, I had been taught to squash insects because they were pests, and inconsequential. I began to realize that my attitude was not only arrogant and human-centric but also ultimately destructive, because all living things—plant, animal, insect—are so interrelated that the welfare of the whole depends on the health of each. I learned to see insects not as pests but as part of the food chain that keeps our ecosystem in balance. If a particular insect population grows too large, something is wrong; it means the equilibrium has been disrupted and needs to be brought back into balance.

Walking in the vineyard became a nature walk, and I relished everything I saw. As I walked among the vines, I watched dragonflies traveling around the grape canopy and heard the background hum of bees. I would come across one of our six feral but cautiously friendly cats—I dubbed them our Rodent Patrol—sitting perfectly still, watching the fresh dirt of an active gopher mound, ready to pounce. Right above me, swallows soared and dived to grab small insects out of the air. Higher up a hawk circled, probably eyeing a mouse. Often I would see a majestic great blue heron fly over. I felt a vibrancy in the vineyard I hadn't felt since the early years. Biodiversity had given it new life and energy.

The LIVE program did not mandate organic practices, but for me organic farming was the next step. Why use any synthetic chemicals that would kill the ecosystem we were trying to encourage? Federal standards had recently been put in place, and *organic* was, at that point, a legal term. Farms and products could not claim to be organic unless they were certified. Going after organic certification would be a big decision. It would mean I could no longer use the synthetic products we had traditionally used to kill mildew and rot. I would have to give up Roundup, the best chemical we had for killing unwanted growth under the vines. While I was considering this step, I joined a small group of local winegrowers to study biodynamic farming—a program that Rudolf Steiner had developed in the 1920s, based on cosmology, that timed farming practices to the movement of the moon and planets. Many of its precepts were so far out of our thinking framework that they seemed outlandish, but we knew that some of the greatest vineyards in Europe were farmed biodynamically, and we tried hard to understand.

The fervor I felt for the environment—what we had done to it and what we needed to do to resuscitate it—was much on my mind. The problem was far bigger than my vineyard, but I had contributed to the damage, and I could contribute to the renewal. By the early 2000s, I was on a mission to change, and change quickly. I hired a consultant who was a successful biodynamic and organic horticulturalist. His solution to protecting my vines from mildew was compost tea, which he taught me how to brew. He designed and built a brewer that steeped compost in water and then circulated it through a series of free-form vessels. He had devised the pear shape of the vessels, he said, from the shape of his wife's pregnant torso. The whole contraption, about six feet high, sat over a large trough full of water and looked like a multilayered fountain. Circulation aerated the tea and encouraged the rapid growth of microorganisms. In forty-eight hours the brew was ready, and we sprayed it on the vine canopy in the two blocks we had chosen for the experiment. The theory was that the microbial activity in the tea would set up enough competition on the grape leaves to keep any one organism from dominating. Mildew and other disease organisms would be held in check.

After my vineyard manager had made the tea and sprayed it several times, he suddenly called me, over the Fourth of July weekend, in a panic. "Susan," he said, "We have a problem. I found mildew in the Bluebird Block. I think we need to spray Rally [the current synthetic chemical for mildew]." I vetoed Rally and told him to try two other sprays that I knew were organically certified. Nothing worked. The mildew got worse and worse, until it became the worst outbreak I had ever seen. As I watched its white sheen spread through the canopy, I knew my two experimental blocks were at risk. I finally caved in and allowed a chemical spray. The berries, canes, and leaves turned from white to black, indicating that the mildew was no longer active.

It was a major setback. In my eagerness to get to where I wanted to be, I had endangered my vines and spoiled the crop from those blocks. Using a synthetic chemical had delayed possible organic certification by another year. Humbled and chagrined, I realized I needed to move more slowly and make the transition to organic farming in stages. My vines needed time to learn to grow on their own, without the crutch of chemicals. Going too fast was like taking a patient off life support before his system was ready. My consultant was very apologetic, but we parted ways. Being sorry doesn't help when the damage is irreversible. The Bluebird Block never fully recovered, and a few years later we removed the vines.

The concept of working with nature felt so right that I badly wanted it to show positive results, and soon. But after that incident, I moved more slowly. After studying biodynamic principles for a year, visiting biodynamic vineyards in California, and seeing how biodynamic farming took organic farming to the next level, I decided to try biodynamic practices on our two blocks of Pinot Gris, a total of seven acres. I had some time, after our mildew fiasco, to think about whether I really wanted to be certified organic, since application could not be made until I had farmed chemical-free for one year. I sent for the application from the United States Department of Agriculture (USDA), just to see what was required. The leap between claiming to farm organically and going after certification was large. There was extensive record-keeping involved, it required finding ways to prevent contamination from neighboring farms, and it eliminated irrevocably the possibility of using chemicals.

I dallied in filling out the cumbersome application forms, which required five years of records and extensive explanations of every farm input. But with a final burst of energy and determination, I completed it all and sent in the inch-thick application. After a lengthy review and inspection, we entered our three-year transition to full organic certification. Sixty vineyards were in the LIVE program by then, but organically certified vineyards were few. When we received our certification in 2005, several small Oregon vineyards (two to ten acres) were certified, but only seven (out of three hundred) Oregon wineries with vineyards had made the USDA list. They were Bergstrom Vineyards, Brick House Vineyards, Cooper Mountain Vineyards, Evesham Wood Vineyard, King Estate Winery, Lemelson Vineyards, and Sokol Blosser.

I also began to understand that sustainability applied to more than farming. I began applying the principles of sustainability to our entire business as a result of a workshop Russ and I attended in April 1999 about a new program that had been developed in Sweden, called The Natural Step. The name made it sound like an orthopedic shoe company, but the concept ignited a small fire in my brain. The Natural Step program is directed toward universal sustainability. Based on accepted scientific principles, it addresses our relationship with the physical universe and offers a framework of system conditions under which all human action should take place. Those system conditions focus on rectifying the systematic degradation of the environment that occurs when we use natural resources (petroleum, coal) faster than they can be created, turn these resources into products that don't decompose (plastics), and create waste that has nowhere to go in the closed system that is our planet. After learning about The Natural Step, I began to apply the principles of sustainability not just to our farming practices but to all phases of operation at Sokol Blosser. Considered in this broader light, our degree of unsustainabilty was horrifying, and almost overwhelming.

How naive I had been, all the while thinking of myself as an environmentalist. I looked at the nonrenewable resources we used and saw how dominated my business was by unsustainable practices. Eliminating synthetic chemicals and fertilizers and farming organically was a small start. Sustainability was a much bigger concept. Black plastic under our new plantings for weed suppression and water retention eliminated herbicide use, but it also meant using a nonrecyclable petroleum product. The tin capsules and metallic labels we used in our packaging looked upscale and classy but were not the most sustainable options. We stocked our tasting room with bleached paper products and ran ream after ream of virgin paper through the copiers and printers. We did it without thinking; it was the usual way things were done. Once I realized the implications, I knew we had to change. I began the long, slow process of educating myself and my employees and scrutinizing each part of the operation. We soon had the chance to put our new principles to work on a major project: building a new wine cellar.

⁘

We had tackled two of the three crucial components of winemaking—winemaker and grapes—and had made a start with the third, technology, with our new press, stemmer, and grape-handling equipment. Now we had to face the issue we had put off because of the huge capital outlay we foresaw: barrel storage for the Pinot Noir. We had two issues, storage conditions and storage space. Our winery building was too hot in summer, too cold in winter, and never humid enough to prevent excess evaporation through the French oak barrels. And because we intended to double our Pinot Noir production, we would need room for more barrels as soon as our new plantings started producing.

We looked at every option and finally admitted that the most efficient solution would be to build new barrel storage adjacent to the winery. We had no budget for architectural flourishes, but decided we would try to follow the precepts of The Natural Step and build it sustainably. Bill suggested we look at the U.S. Green Building Council's new certification program, which sets strict guidelines for sustainable building. We had started with an architect who had winery but no "green" experience. We decided to switch to a firm that specialized in sustainable building, SERA Architects, and Russ worked closely with them for the next year. The simple structure that resulted belied the amount of thought behind it, and its complex underpinnings. Dug into the hillside, the cellar had a low profile and a rounded top covered with three feet of soil that was quickly rampant with wildflowers of every color, adding to the biodiversity of the vineyard. In its 5,200 square feet of silent, humid darkness, the barrels could age at a constant 55 to 60 degrees Fahrenheit year-round without any air-conditioning. For meeting its strict siting, energy, water, materials, and waste criteria, the U.S. Green Building Council awarded us its esteemed LEED (Leadership in Energy and Environmental Design) Silver 2.0 certification. We were the first winery in the country to achieve this distinction. Sustainable construction was so far out of the mainstream at that time that it took substantial extra effort to make it happen. The LEED certification meant a lot to me, and I made sure the large silver plaque we received got installed on a post positioned prominently at the entrance to the new cellar.

The building had caused a lot of talk in the industry, so we held an open house. Governor Ted Kulongoski, who had made sustainability a priority in his new administration, came and spoke, as did Secretary of State Bill Bradbury, the head of his Sustainability Task Force. The governor stood against a backdrop of French oak barrels full of Pinot Noir, on a platform made that morning of wine pallets, and began by telling the gathering, "Twenty-five years ago, Bill and Susan put wine in a bottle, and Oregon has been better off since." He had been well briefed. His speech delighted the guests, and all of the Sokol Blosser family wore big smiles. Christine Ervin, the president of the U.S. Green Building Council, told the gathering that only thirty-seven projects in the United States had achieved LEED certification, although more than eight hundred had registered. I had met with her the preceding year to discuss the certification requirements and

*The barrel cellar, with its wildflowers and grasses on top and lavender,
Russian sage, yarrow, and other beneficial-insect-attracting plants at each end,
became part of our biodiversity program. (Photo by Doreen L. Wynja.)*

to scope out the obstacles, and I had left our meeting discouraged but not totally flattened. At the open house, she told me that when we did decide to take on the challenge, she had thought to herself, *If anyone can make this happen, it's Susan.* She'd had faith in me that I hadn't had in myself.

Sokol Blosser was the first winery and the first agricultural project to achieve LEED certification, but sustainable building, while rare, was not new. Notable wineries in California, such as Fetzer and Sanford, had followed sustainable principles in their buildings. In Oregon, the Carlton Winemakers Studio had followed LEED principles, though the group had not pursued certification. As the concept of sustainability became more widespread, newer wineries embraced it. Stoller Winery announced its intention to go after LEED certification when building a winery across the road from the old farmhouse we had first rented, where the turkey sheds had once been.

While I led the drive toward sustainability at the vineyards and winery, these were heartfelt values shared by my family, especially Bill and Nik, as well as Russ, whose uncompromising sustainability ethic kept us moving in the right direction. After Bill turned over the winery presidency to me, his planning career focused on issues of sustainability, and talking with him about his work was my introduction to the subject. Nik's career now had a similar focus. He and a friend had started their own environmental publishing company. They were putting out coupon books for sustainable products in three major cities: the *Chinook Book* in Portland and Seattle, and the *Blue Sky Guide* in Minneapolis. One day, Nik asked me if I would be interested in a publication that talked about sustainability in various areas of business. I told him it would have to be really good; I already had too many unread publications on my desk. He made it his goal to formulate a periodical that his mom would like so much she would pay to read it. When the *Sustainable Industries Journal,* a compendium of sustainable activity in various sectors of the economy of the Northwest appeared, I was dumb-founded to discover the scope of activity and the variety of business are-nas. I subscribed, read my copy every month as soon as it arrived, and always learned something new and useful. I couldn't believe he had done it.

As we were working toward sustainability at the winery, the term was entering the business lexicon but wasn't yet in vogue. I never regretted the extra trouble, time, and expense our commitment entailed. After a while, I was surprised and gratified to discover how interested people were in what we were doing. Not everyone cared, but those who did let us know. We slowly integrated our values into our marketing program.

⁘

My business life might have been active, but my personal life came to a standstill when I left Bill. I had no interest in meeting single men or replac-ing my marriage with another relationship. Between travel and hosting win-ery guests, I had a small social life. Marsha Palanci came to visit the winery in January, right after I had moved out, and I surprised her at the airport with the news that she would be staying in my new apartment. She was my first visitor, and I was glad to be with a friend in my tender emotional state.

I couldn't imagine having a "date," and matchmaking of any kind, through friends or the Internet, sounded abhorrent. I spent time with female friends, or, if I wanted company for an event or a movie, I asked Russ to go with me. He seemed so clearly a loner, I knew he hadn't met many people in the area and probably wouldn't on his own. I appointed myself his local travel guide, and together we visited Portland's museums and public gardens.

When I hired Russ, I saw him as serious, cautious, and focused — qualities that drew me to him as a winemaker. When we worked together,

I appreciated his willingness to answer when I tentatively posed the sort of questions about winemaking that previous winemakers, and even Bill, had treated with condescension. For the first time, I felt welcome in the cellar. When I complained about the difficulties I was having putting together new ten-year projections for the winery, Russ showed me spreadsheet techniques that made my work simpler. He seemed content to go home and be alone, but I pursued him; he was one of the few people I enjoyed being with. I had discovered that the sharp mind and gruff exterior protected a warm heart and hid a riotous sense of humor. There was a lot more to Russ than he let people see, and I found myself wanting to know him better. We started spending more and more time together, apart from work.

Who can fathom the human heart? Just when I had come to terms with never having another relationship, one happened. I worried that I was on the rebound from Bill, but I rationalized that I had been grieving my failed relationship with Bill for years, and that the actual break had been cathartic. Right or wrong, once Russ and I each overcame our doubts, we let ourselves go, and entered a heady affair that consumed us both. A lifetime of pent-up feelings came pouring out. I loved as I had never loved before. I was awed at its power. Russ felt the same intensity. We became inseparable; I didn't want to do anything he wasn't part of. When I traveled alone for business, I wrote him poems, puerile and passionate. He was my other half and I plunged on, knowing I was breaking every rule in the book by having an affair with my winemaker.

We were circumspect at work and at industry events, but when it became clear to me that Russ and I had a relationship that went far beyond employer-employee and was not just temporary, I knew I had to tell the other winery owners, especially Bill. I was nervous when I called Bill and arranged to meet him for a drink in Portland. I expected him to berate me for being stupid enough to get involved with an employee, and I steeled myself for the onslaught. Instead, he said, "I'm happy for you," and acted like he meant it. It helped that he was in a new relationship as well, and he told me about her. I couldn't believe it had gone so well; I breathed a big sigh of relief.

The reaction of my children caught me by surprise. All three, when I told them, acted shocked and dumbfounded. "What do you think you're doing?" they cried. My husband, from whom I was separated but not yet divorced, had accepted the news better than our kids, who, with varying degrees of hysteria, scolded me as if they were the parents and I the child. I called Eugenia, who knew about my new relationship. "Eugenia, my kids don't approve of me," I told her.

"What are you doing about it?" she asked.

"I'm avoiding them," I confessed.

I had to pull the phone away from my ear, she hooted so loudly. When she got over laughing at the role reversal, she advised me to deal with it and talk to them. I felt very fragile emotionally, but I finally sat down with them and asked them to give me the same freedom to make mistakes that I had given them when they were falling in love. I reminded them how I had supported their decisions. They thought back. "Oh, yeah," they said. "You did."

I also told them I knew the dangers of starting a relationship with Russ, and I would not let it hurt the winery. My friend Heidi Yorkshire, who couldn't believe how happy I looked, told them, "Look how in love your mother is. Let her be. Be happy for her." It all helped.

On my next trip to New York, Marsha and I had dinner with Marguerite Thomas, whom I hadn't seen for more than a year. I told them what had been happening, and especially how surprised I was that my adult kids were having so much difficulty with all the changes, including my new relationship. Marguerite understood immediately. Her husband had died several years before; she was now in a new relationship, and her grown kids were also acting like disapproving parents. Did we have to give up someone we loved because our kids, who had left home and had their own lives, objected? We agreed that we had to live our own lives, too. There we were, two middle-aged women in an elegant midtown Manhattan restaurant, commiserating over architecturally arranged vegetables, Asian noodles, and Sokol Blosser wine, sounding more like teenagers at a drive-in, talking about how their stupid parents restricted their freedom.

By the end of the year, Russ and I and YumYum were settled into a house Russ and I had bought together, about twenty minutes from the winery. I was happier and more at peace inside than I had ever been. Our relationship went against all common sense, all rules for business success, and all conventions of employer-employee interaction. I was never at ease working side by side with Bill, yet I loved working with Russ. His passionate drive for quality was my gyroscope at work. We maintained a business relationship at the winery and work-related events—he was the winemaker, I was the winery owner. Just being together made work special. I never anticipated, and could not have imagined when I hired him, that Russ would be part of not only the winery's renaissance, but also mine.

The winery's revitalization at the end of the 1990s and start of the new century was, meanwhile, being supported by an upward surge in the local industry as a whole. Wine buyers across the country were requesting Oregon wine, especially Pinot Noir but increasingly Pinot Gris as well, for restaurant wine lists and retail wine shelves. Newer wineries, especially those with a lot of marketing money, gave Oregon more visibility in the marketplace. Higher-quality and more consistent wines gave Oregon better press. Oregon had become a destination for wine lovers—still far behind California, but growing fast. Our tasting room was open seven days a week all year, closed only for Thanksgiving Day, Christmas Day, and New Year's Day. For a long time, tasting-room visitors had provided the greatest revenue for consumer-direct sales. Then, during the 1990s, new options helped us boost retail sales.

Historically, the retail part of our business depended on customers coming in person to our tasting room. Laws forbidding wine shipment across most state borders hampered mail-order sales and made interstate shipment a hot-button issue in the industry. It divided two groups that worked together on most issues, wineries and distributors. The wineries lobbied for the freedom to ship into any state; distributors were actively against it. The distributors had better organization and more financial clout, but the wineries gradually got organized and took the issue through the courts, contending that the laws infringed on commerce and created unfair competition by favoring in-state wineries. Change started slowly but then picked up steam. The number of states into which we could legally ship wine increased from five to twenty-six within six years, increasing direct sales considerably. We knew the barriers would come down eventually and the direct shipment market would explode. We wanted to be prepared. It wasn't until the issue reached the U.S. Supreme Court that the armor started to crack. After the Supreme Court's favorable decision in 2005, formerly intransigent states voluntarily opened up, and we were glad to be ready.

In 1997, we created our Cellar Club to provide regular wine shipments to members. As more states allowed direct shipment, we added more members. This growing group of loyal customers inspired us to put on member tastings, dinners, cooking classes, vineyard walks, blending parties, and other special events, as well as to offer member discounts.

Then came the Internet—a giant boost to consumer-direct sales, after

people became comfortable using it. When the Internet first started to gar-
ner attention, we were invited, in 1996, to join an informational Web site
that became a Web marketplace for local businesses. As the Internet got
more sophisticated, so did we. We created www.sokolblosser.com, added
secure sales capability, redesigned our site every few years, and updated
monthly. The Internet came of age as a sales and public-relations tool in a
few years, demonstrating how fast technology could modify the marketplace. The Internet, Web sites, e-mail—all beyond our imagination when
Sokol Blosser started—became increasingly vital to our business.

Retail was an important subcategory, but three-quarters of our sales
were still through wholesalers. For almost twenty years, more than half of
all wholesale sales came from within Oregon, but by the late 1990s that
had changed. Growth was in the national arena, and even with Alex's help,
it was too much for us to handle. The two of us simply couldn't be out in
the market as much as we needed to be. We talked a lot about what the
next step should be. We had four brokers who represented us in different
markets, and we didn't know whether to expand that program, hire our
own traveling salesperson, or be on the road more ourselves. Nothing
seemed just right.

Fate stepped in one wintry day in 1999 when Bill Terlato of Paterno
Imports, which had a portfolio of prominent international wines, called
to say that his firm had been looking at Sokol Blosser and wanted to rep-
resent us. I agreed to meet with him, but I wasn't optimistic. We hadn't
done too well through Bob Haas and Vineyard Brands, though they had
tried hard, and the next national marketing group had done even worse. I
couldn't imagine how this one would be different.

I showed Bill Terlato and two of his vice presidents around the winery.
I pointed out our new equipment and explained our vision of higher quality, showed them where we would be planting more Pinot Noir, and told

them about the new cellar that would allow us to expand production. They nodded and asked if we could sit down and talk. We had no conference room, so we went to my office. It was a good-size room whose major piece of furniture was my large wood-veneer desk, recently acquired on sale at Staples. Aside from that, my office resembled a used furniture store with its mismatched pieces. A huge burlap-covered bulletin board of photos, newspaper articles, memorabilia, and *New Yorker* cartoons covered the largest wall. On a narrow shelf under the clerestory windows, a long row of dusty wine bottles displayed our various labels and wines over the years. Those three perfectly coiffed men, in their Italian suits and shirts with monogrammed cuffs, who had flown in on a private corporate jet, now settled themselves on straight-backed metal chairs across from me at my conference table—a folding six-foot table with a chipped fake-wood veneer. I fitted right into the decor in my standard winter garb of jeans, turtleneck sweater, and fleece vest. The scene's incongruity did not keep us from serious discussion.

I challenged Bill Terlato to explain what he could do for us, and he talked about their vision of representing a limited number of high-end wineries. He encouraged me to talk with the other wineries he represented and visit his headquarters in Illinois. I put it on the back burner for several months. Finally, in April, on my way to the East Coast, I stopped at the Paterno headquarters, Tangley Oaks. My first surprise was that I had been there before. It was the old Armour estate, where my mother and I had once attended an antiques show. I spent the day in the mansion with the Terlato team, and they said all the right things to impress me. The next morning, when I telephoned Alan Dreeben, my Texas distributor friend who I knew carried the Paterno portfolio, he told me he thought a small winery like ours really needed someone like Paterno to assure that we got attention. Although we still had to travel to maintain our personal connections to the marketplace, Paterno soon provided the national distribution network that we had not been able to achieve on our own.

⁘

During much of the 1990s, Oregon wineries worked together through the Oregon Wine Marketing Coalition (OWMC) to promote their wines nationally. We had seen how successfully Napa wineries had cooperated to gain national attention, with trade shows and consumer tastings in major cities, and we decided we needed to do the same. Paul Hart from Rex Hill Vineyards got us organized, and the OWMC did much to increase our national visibility. By 1999, most of the major cities had been visited. Pat Dudley of Bethel Heights Vineyard, the OWMC president, looking for the best way to publicize the highly touted 1998 vintage, wondered: Why not bring the key wine buyers to Oregon wine country, so they can experience it for themselves? This turned out to be an idea whose time had come.

A few of the Oregon winery owners who had been involved with the International Pinot Noir Celebration (IPNC), which had survived and prospered for a dozen years, had been wondering whether it was time to create an Oregon-only Pinot Noir event. Was the world now ready for Oregon Pinot Noir, all by itself, without the lure of Burgundy? A recent tour for the international Masters of Wine, organized and led by Portland wine writer Lisa Shara Hall, had been very positively received by all involved. Pat Dudley and Dave Adelsheim organized a meeting to discuss three key questions: Did Oregon have enough prestige to draw people to an event featuring only Oregon wine? Should this be a Pinot Noir event? Who exactly did we want to come? The meeting's attendees—Dave Adelsheim, Pat Dudley, Nancy Ponzi, Karen Wright, Danielle Andrus, Diana Lett, Harry

Peterson-Nedry, myself, and a few others—finally settled on what we thought was just the right concept.

We took the IPNC model and pared it back to an invitation-only, trade-only event—no consumers or media. Our goal was to attract the key wine-buyers from the best restaurants and wine stores all over the country, let them experience the beauty of Oregon wine country and the quality of the wines, and convince them to put more Oregon wine on their shelves and wine lists. We decided to emphasize Pinot Noir; it was what Oregon was known for and would capture attention. We fashioned a three-day program of vineyard and winery visits, tastings, workshops, and gourmet meals that highlighted Oregon's bounty. In line with our informal, unslick style, David and Diana Lett suggested that we call this adventure Oregon Pinot Camp.

The board, composed of winery principals, got a grant from the Oregon Wine Advisory Board and hired Sue Horstmann, who had years of event planning experience and, most recently, had been a Yamhill County Wineries Association staffer. Our boardroom was the Dundee Bistro, a restaurant that had been started by the Ponzi family and had become the unofficial meeting place for conducting local wine-industry business. All of us had been deeply involved with IPNC, and Pat Dudley, like me, had been its director for several years. It had taught us how to put on a successful event.

We spent almost a year planning the Oregon Pinot Camp; the first campers arrived in late June 2000, just as the grape clusters burst into bloom. We divided them into groups and took them around in yellow school buses to workshops and tastings at different wineries. Campers saw more of the local scenery than we intended because the bus drivers often got hopelessly lost trying to find wineries on unmarked back roads. Still, all went off as planned, and we were heartily applauded. Each evening, the campers and winery principals convened for dinner under a big white tent at one of the larger wineries. The high-level wine-buyers, sommeliers, chefs, and store owners got to know their peers from across the country, and they loved it. A feeling of camaraderie suffused the tent. As we heaped our plates with gourmet salads and fresh wild salmon grilled over an open pit fire, drank Pinot Noir, and watched the sun set over the vineyards, we knew that Oregon wine country had been finely drawn in our campers' minds.

Campers told us they couldn't wait to return to camp next year. Surprise spread across their faces when we told them they couldn't. But we were serious. We wanted a new crop of campers every year so we could continue to introduce more people to Oregon. We realized we would need to start another program for our camper alumni. The OPC, as it was nicknamed, was such a smashing success that top wine people all over the country started asking how they could get an invitation. It became a badge of honor to be an OPC alumnus. The wine press, used to being coddled and catered to, pleaded to be allowed to attend.

The triumph of OPC gave winemakers who had built their reputations as employees the courage to start their own operations. Lynn Penner-Ash from Rex Hill Vineyards, Sam Tannahill from Archery Summit, Rob Stuart from Erath Vineyards, and Laurent Montalieu from WillaKenzie Estate all left employment about the same time. Well-known California winemakers, like Tony Soter, gravitated north to Oregon. And a new wave of young urban professionals bought land to pursue their dreams of owning vineyards and making wine. Oregon labels I had never heard of appeared on wine lists and retail shelves. Dave Adelsheim, Nancy Ponzi, Diana Lett, and I sat together on the board of OPC, looked at the unfamiliar names of all the Oregon wineries that wanted to participate, and reminisced about the days when the whole industry fitted into one living room. Almost thirty years had gone by. Although the memory was as vivid as only yesterday, it was a bygone era. Oregon now contained almost three hundred wineries and fourteen thousand acres of wine grapes, 60 percent of which were devoted to Pinot Noir.

Oregon Pinot Camp was a tribute to the willingness of Oregon wineries to collaborate. We recognized that, while we were ultimately selling against one another, our primary competition was wine from other regions, especially California. Promoting Oregon helped all of us. Oregon teamwork was one of the most talked-about aspects of OPC; campers couldn't believe that we worked together as well as we did. The tradition of collaboration that had started in the 1970s was being passed on to the newcomers.

⁝⁝

Activity on another front also aimed at drawing attention to Oregon wine: we were working to secure appellations that would highlight the various growing regions within the Willamette Valley. Appellation on a wine bottle tells the consumer where the grapes came from, and the narrower the designation, the more precisely the vineyard locations are pinpointed. In 2000, the most precise federal appellation available for our vineyards was "Willamette Valley," a huge area 120 miles long and 25 to 40 miles wide. Bill and I had wanted to be able to give our wines a Red Hills of Dundee appellation in the 1970s, and Bill had proposed applying for it, but growers outside the Red Hills area had protested. At that time, Dave Adelsheim strongly believed that appellations were premature and might tear us into small competing groups at a time when we needed to hang together. Applying for a particular region to be designated as an American Viticultural Area (AVA)—the prerequisite for using an appellation on a label—was a major undertaking that involved detailed formal petitions to the federal Bureau of Alcohol, Tobacco, and Firearms (BATF; now known as the Alcohol and Tobacco Tax and Trade Bureau, or TTB). Bill gave the project up, since opposition made acceptance by the federal government almost impossible.

Twenty-five years later, Alex decided to see if perhaps the time had come to try again. Instead of going after just the appellation we wanted, Alex called around, found other winery owners interested in getting appellations for their areas, and convened the group. His idea was that the growers of different potential appellations would work together, and that the process would unite rather than divide us. He called and visited the old guard—David Lett, Dick Erath, Dick Ponzi, Dave Adelsheim—to get their blessings and, he hoped, their active support. Dave Adelsheim was the last holdout, but he finally agreed that the time was right to go after smaller AVAs. Dave, Harry Peterson-Nedry, Rollin Soles, Ted Casteel, Russ Rainey, Ken Wright, and Alex formed the active steering committee and led the way for the resulting six appellation applications, all representing areas within the northern part of the Willamette Valley. The original thought was that because the new AVAs had distinct soil profiles, such as the Dundee Hills red clay loam, soils would serve as their distinction. But we learned that the federal government cared only about the historical authenticity of the name and clear boundary delineation, so those issues became the focus of discussion.

Since Alex called the meetings and served as secretary of the steering committee, he was the one people called with complaints. During the process of getting consensus from all the wineries and vineyards in the region, he spent considerable time responding to issues. His desk was not far away from mine, and I could hear him on the phone. First, there would be an extended silence punctuated by his expressions of compassion. Then he would ask questions aimed at uncovering the real concern. Often the caller wanted simply to be heard, to have a voice. I was in awe of his patience and diplomacy.

After more than a year of discussion and compromise, the leaders of the six appellation groups submitted their petitions to the government. The name Red Hills of Dundee had been changed to Dundee Hills to avoid any potential conflict with a simultaneous petition from California that contained the words *Red Hills*. The Dundee Hills application was written by Alex and Rollin Soles, the Chehalem Mountains application by Dave Adelsheim, Ribbon Ridge by Harry Peterson-Nedry, Eola Hills by Russ Raney and Ted Casteel, Yamhill-Carlton District by Ken Wright, and McMinnville by Kevin Byrd. The wait began. People told us the approval process would take a minimum of three years and could last for many more if there were controversy. The applications slowly wended their way through the federal bureaucracy, an obstacle course in any case but made even more difficult by agency changes as the BATF morphed into the TTB. Even with no opposition, the process seemed to take forever. Finally, in October 2004 it was announced that the Dundee Hills appellation had won final approval and would be available for use after January 31, 2005. McMinnville and Yamhill-Carlton were approved soon after. Eola Hills and Chehalem Mountains got bogged down in controversy because existing wineries had those names, and had to await a negotiated compromise.

We had delayed printing labels, hoping to be able to use the new appellation, and approval came just in time. Sokol Blosser's 2002 Pinot Noirs, released in March 2005, became the first Oregon wines to carry the Dundee Hills appellation. Alex had successfully finished what his father had initiated.

While the AVA applications were being written, the market for high-end wine was contracting. We saw our Pinot Noir sales slipping. The economic recession that followed the dot-com crash in 2000 and the September 11, 2001, terrorist attack created panic in the market as inventories built up. Needing a short-term fix, many wineries slashed their prices to make

The first Dundee Hills appellation on the market, Sokol Blosser's
2002 Dundee Hills Pinot Noir (left); the revised Evolution
label (right), as Evolution No. 9 became simply Evolution.
(Photos by Alter Image, courtesy of Paterno Wines International.)

sales. Pinot Noir was still a small niche, compared to Cabernet Sauvignon or Chardonnay, and while demand for Oregon Pinot Noir was growing, the supply was growing faster than the demand, especially in the over-twenty-five-dollar category that included Sokol Blosser. As competition increased, we saw wineries in California, Oregon, and Washington close their doors, some selling and others simply going out of business.

Alex and I realized we were depending too much on Paterno. We were in a person-to-person business, and to increase sales we both needed to travel more, renew old friendships, and make new ones. Besides, we had a story to tell. We needed to be out talking about the renaissance at Sokol Blosser—our new vineyards, our new barrel cellar, the high-quality wines that our new winemaker was creating.

We both got out on the road, Alex reluctant to leave his new twin sons and I thinking this was déjà vu all over again—working the market, lunching with the trade, hosting winery dinners for consumers, meeting with the press, contacting one potential account after another. Travel was exhausting, but it also felt good seeing buyers again. And we saw sales improve in the markets we visited.

A day working the market still meant crisscrossing town for consecutive appointments with wine buyers. It wasn't unusual for the person to be too busy to see us, or for us to have to bide our time in a line of sales reps, all with wine bags full of samples. Everyone wanted to sit down with the wine buyer, pour tastes, and leave with an order. I had days when every account bought and days when I didn't sell one bottle. Neither result really indicated what that buyer might do the next day, or the next month.

My favorite way of meeting with prospective buyers has always been to host a lunch where I could talk to several buyers at once and have their full attention. At their workplaces, they were too easily distracted. Those luncheons became a key sales tool, and sometimes everything came together just right. One of those times was a luncheon for sommeliers and wine press I hosted in Dallas, in a historic house now famous as the Mansion on Turtle Creek. When I arrived, an hour early, to check on everything, I was shown to a private corner room with six arched glass doors on each outside wall. The room had plum-colored walls with gold-and-white-striped wallpaper below the wainscoting, a massive wrought-iron chandelier, and a floor of polished tile. The sun, filtering through the trees, shone on the six empty wineglasses at each of the twelve places and shimmered on the cut crystal vases that held single roses. The server told us the lovely space had been the breakfast room of the old house.

I opened and tasted each of the six wines we would be pouring to make sure they were all sound. The maître d' brought a menu so I could choose the right match with the wines. I selected a crabmeat, avocado, macadamia nut, and pink grapefruit salad to match the Pinot Gris, but asked them to leave out the grapefruit, which brought too much acid to the dish. To show off the versatility of the four Pinot Noirs, I chose a seared scallop and smoked duck dish. For dessert, I requested a simple cheese plate, including blue cheese. The saltiness would go perfectly with my dessert Riesling.

I placed packets of information and small gifts—a Sokol Blosser corkscrew and a Noir Bar, made by Oregon's Dagoba Organic Chocolate to go with our Pinot Noir—at each place. Then I sat back and waited. I felt wrung out; Dallas was the fourth city in four days, but I knew the guests' arrival would trigger an adrenalin rush.

When everyone was seated, I stood up, smiled at my guests, and said I was pleased to be there to tell them in person about the changes at Sokol Blosser. And I was. I had a story to tell—Sokol Blosser had reinvented itself.

8

Horizon

As president, I was responsible for, and had a hand in, every part of our operation. That's the nature of small business—to be continually switching hats. Mine was not exactly a series of hats, but more like a hard hat with a rotating spotlight. The light swiveled from vineyard to wine production, tasting room, distributor sales, Internet, public relations, finances, facility maintenance, and landscaping. It picked up speed as my attention shifted. Some days, it was more like the beacon on a police car, rotating so fast it lit up everything at once.

Every day had its share of surprises: An important buyer dropped in without notice. We were asked to participate in an imaginative fund-raiser for one of our favorite causes. Something we couldn't live without broke down—the tasting room's glass-washer, tank refrigeration, computer system. An unexpected order came in from one of our export markets. Mildew was found in the vineyard. A wine writer on deadline needed a phone interview right away. One of the cats needed to go immediately to the vet. I loved every one of my areas of responsibility and thrived on the variety.

Finances got daily attention; what I learned from our income, cash flow, and balance statements set new sales and marketing initiatives in motion. Keeping up with current sales was essential to planning future production. I had a rolling five-year pro forma that I continually updated and revised.

Every day included some writing—the president's newsletter for a Cellar Club shipment, a paragraph about the winery for a festival or tasting, updates for the staff and board, or a new handout or brochure. I never ran out of things to do. When complacency threatened, something new would always come along to shake things up. Often I just answered my phone to find someone with an interesting new idea or project on the other end.

I gave up doing the physical vineyard work when I took over the presidency in 1991, but my heart was still in the vineyards, and I worked closely with Luis Hernandez, my vineyard manager. Luis proved to me that the American Dream is alive and well. He came from a small Mexican village, La Joya, in Guanajuato, and grew up carrying buckets of water to cemeteries to water the graveside flowers for wealthy people, earning a peso per bucket. He was a migrant worker in California before coming to Oregon. We had hired him in the 1980s on a recommendation from Putt at Putt's Market in Dayton. Luis had gone through a migrant education program and could read and write English, as well as speak it. We had a good relationship. Over the years, I had bailed him out of jail when he was caught driving after too much beer; seen him settle down, marry a woman from his hometown, and raise four children; and watched him grow into a manager who could keep more than one crew on task and Sokol Blosser's vineyard looking good. Every December and January, Luis went back to Mexico to see his mother and work on his retirement house. I was always relieved to see him come back. All of his crew came from his town, and most were related. The ones who didn't have families with them lived in a house Luis owned in McMinnville. We set aside and fenced a large area next to our equipment shed for his crew to keep a vegetable garden. Before and after work I would see them hoeing the corn and peppers and watering the tomatillos.

Early morning was the best time for Luis and me to go out in the vineyard to check for bloom or mildew (our most persistent disease problem) or color change or crop load. I trusted Luis's experience and instincts, but I wanted to be the final decision-maker. As we transitioned to organic farming, I located and procured the special supplies — organic cow manure and straw, organic cover-crop seed, biodynamic preparations, and botanical sprays — that we needed for our compost, our cover crops, and our biodynamic experiment. My office shelves held an expanding number of large loose-leaf binders that stored the extensive vineyard records that both LIVE and Oregon Tilth, the USDA's organic certifying agency, required.

Every year, as harvest approached, I thought about the rain-soaked harvest of 1984 and wondered what the upcoming harvest would bring. Russ, Luis, and I made a joint decision about when to harvest each block, after walking through the vineyard and tasting the grapes many times. None of us ever knew for sure what the perfect time was. Experience had trained us to focus on rain and its potential effect; moisture damage was our biggest fear. As a result, the heat and drought of 2003 caught us, and all the wine-growers, totally off guard. It was as dramatic as the harvest of 1984, with the weather reversed.

The 2003 season started out with an unusually wet spring. Twenty-eight consecutive days of rain in March and April set new records. Then, as if someone turned the faucet off and the heat lamp on, there was no measurable rain during June, July, and August. We had unseasonably hot weather, with the temperature above ninety degrees for days and occasionally climbing close to one hundred. That kind of heat might be common in California, but our cool-weather vines hated the hot weather as much as we did. The leaves on our thirty-two acres of unirrigated young vines pulled inward, as if protecting themselves. They didn't have the deep root systems of the older vines, so they had more trouble coping. We cut the crop back so they would have fewer clusters to keep hydrated and waited for the rain, which was predicted to come at any moment. Rain finally fell in early September, and although it seemed like a downpour, the ground soaked it up so fast that it looked dry the next day. Now we needed, and expected, our classic fall weather—sunny days alternating with short bouts of rain.

The sun came out, and for the next ten days it just got hotter and hotter, peaking at a record ninety-five degrees. A strong east wind exacerbated the heat and exerted a desiccating influence. Our grapes catapulted up the Brix scale—the measure of sugar percentage in wine grapes—and we found clusters with grapes that had started to soften and get wrinkly. Others had actually started to shrivel and would become raisins if the clusters dehydrated. While the sugar level is crucial, it is just one parameter of maturation. The most important one is flavor, and these grapes hadn't had time to develop the complex flavors of maturity.

With no rain in sight, letting the fruit hang longer would only result in more dehydration and higher sugar levels. We were aware that other wineries solved the high sugar-level problem by adding water, but I wasn't willing to permit that. If the Brix got any higher, our wines would end up with unacceptably high alcohol levels. Wine from fruit like this would be dark and powerful, but would it have the elegance and complexity we wanted? We really wouldn't know for almost eighteen months, when we took the wine out of the barrels for bottling.

We knew what we had to do—bring the fruit in—and we reluctantly made the decision to start right away. What an odd problem for Oregon: suffering from too much sun. I hoped it was an anomaly and not an indication of permanent climate change. We immediately called the growers from whom we were buying grapes, and they called us back to report, often with surprise, that their grapes were ready to pick. The near panic at the high Brix levels produced a picking frenzy. Russ faced a logistical nightmare as he orchestrated the picking schedule, arranged for the grape deliveries to come in as fast as we could take them, and allocated fermentation space to each lot of grapes. We revised the picking schedule two or three times a day as we sampled the fruit from our different blocks and got reports from our growers, and then rearranged everything to get the ripest fruit in first. Compounding the confusion, the grapes arrived in amounts that varied from our estimates, forcing Russ to revise again. Russ resembled the harried conductor of an unruly orchestra, trying to keep the players on track with the written music but finding that the flutes, violins, French horns, and cymbals all had their own ideas and played whenever they wanted.

Russ's crush crew numbered five. Two were cellar regulars: our cellarmaster, Doug Vuylsteke, and our cellar worker, Mario Carbajal. Alex, who normally handled sales, and Lee Medina, our tasting room manager, had both cleared their schedules to work harvest, and Marcy, Doug's wife, came on to help. We strove to get our Pinot Noir into fermenters the same day, but first we had to pass the grapes over the conveyor belt and remove the shriveled and raisined clusters, which would give jammy flavors to the wine, and any rotted or underripe fruit. Our small crew accomplished a harvest marathon, processing more than four hundred tons of grapes that just kept coming at them, load after load after load. The last Pinot Noir grapes came in at the end of September, a time that usually saw us just starting our harvest. When it was all over, we realized that we had compressed into fourteen consecutive days a harvest that would normally have stretched over six weeks.

It was one of the earliest harvests on record; the waves of grapes just kept washing up on the winery, while previously scheduled events had to continue as planned. The same Saturday that our crew sorted twenty-one tons of Pinot Noir into fermenters, we hosted a catered dinner at the winery for our Cellar Club members. The following week, we entertained nine Paterno reps who had earned a trip to the winery with their good

sales. They got to help on the sorting line. A local TV station made arrangements to arrive at four-thirty one morning in order to broadcast their morning news show live from Sokol Blosser. It featured an interview with Alex
about the harvest, between news clips and weather. My mother turned
ninety-eight on September 22, so I organized a family birthday dinner; I
can't even remember where it was. Alex couldn't go to our Portland distributor's annual trade tasting because he was busy processing grapes, so
I went, taking bunches of the freshly picked grapes for people to taste. The
long-awaited inspector from Oregon Tilth arrived, and I had to spend half
a day showing him around the vineyard. As much as we would have liked
it to, life didn't stop so we could get through harvest.

After the grapes were in, the vineyard was very still. The chatter of
the pickers, the clattering of the tractors shuffling totes, the raucous jokes
on the sorting line, the blare of the cannon scaring the birds, the beeping
of the forklift backing up on the crush pad—all stopped. We could almost
see the vines sigh with relief that their job was done and they could let themselves close down for the season. What a sense of comfort and accomplish-
ment to open the winery in the morning, seeing and smelling the results
of our work. Rows of small fermenters filled with Pinot Noir grapes actively
fermenting filled the air with their pungent, yeasty grapeyness, the wonderful aroma of a winery during harvest. The vine leaves immediately started
to turn yellow, the first stage as vines go dormant. We all wanted to go
into dormancy, too. Every aspect of the business had been in high gear at
the same time, and we had nearly been flattened by the pace and pressure.

The excitement of new challenges had always renewed my energy, but for
some reason I didn't rebound from the stress of the 2003 harvest. The

demands of the winery began to feel more fatiguing than energizing. I sat at my desk with a million things, large and small, to deal with and no zeal with which to tackle them. What had happened to my old enthusiasm? Was this how Bill had felt back in 1990, before handing over the reins? Maybe I was ready for a change.

Then the internal dialogue began: Was it time for me to give Alex more responsibility? Was he ready? Had I been ready, when Bill and I had switched roles at the end of 1990? Certainly in spirit, but not in management experience. Alex had grown up with the winery, and he had an MBA degree and the business training I hadn't had. But he was barely thirty, and I had been forty-six. I remembered the first time I sat at my desk as winery president and the weight of the responsibility hit me. My insides knotted, realizing that this was where the buck stopped and whatever happened on my watch would be on my conscience. Didn't Alex need more time and more experience before shouldering that weight? Or was that an excuse to hold on to the power I had worked hard to get?

I wondered whether I could give up control gracefully. And if I did step back, how fast and how far back? Bill had stepped out entirely. But he'd been burned out, and I wasn't; I loved the business. I wanted to ease out, turning over day-to-day operations but staying on part-time, more as mentor than advisor, to make sure the right questions were being asked and to oversee the vineyards, watching their health and quality improve with our organic program. Would it work?

Only a few of the pioneering Oregon winery families had successfully brought the second generation into the business, though many had tried. Among our close contemporaries, Dick and Nancy Ponzi seemed to have done the best job, employing their children while they were still active. Joe and Pat Campbell had turned the business over to their son, Adam, and retired, moving out of the area. That was the sum of the success stories so far, though children had recently joined family operations at some later wineries, like Bethel Heights and Lange.

I had three smart, competent kids, any one of whom would be able to rise to the challenge of running the business, but thinking of the strife endemic to family businesses scared me. Articles about families made dysfunctional by rancor, jealousy, and greed appeared periodically in local papers. I couldn't bear to see that happen to my children, who had always gotten along so well.

Turning over what I had created to my adult children, who would continue to build it for their children, held emotional appeal. Was it also good business? All three wanted to keep the business in the family. Nik, while interested and involved as an owner and winery board president, was busy developing his own enterprise. I valued his "outsider's" perspective. Alison, who had just completed her MBA, wrestled with her career choices as she watched her classmates go off to big-bucks jobs at large companies. She tried internships at Nordstrom and Nike, and in the process realized her heart was in the winery. Should she join Alex, and the two of them guide the company? This was a big decision for her, and for the family as well. The family addressed it at board meetings. "This may be the last job you ever have," Alex told her when we offered her a position as director of marketing. After considerable agonizing, she decided to join us at the winery. I think my heart skipped a beat, I was so excited. I had missed her both professionally and personally while she was off at graduate school and other jobs, and was thrilled to have her back permanently.

Alex's commitment to the winery was physical as well as emotional. He and his wife, Jennifer, built a house at the vineyard and moved there in 2003. His sons would grow up as he did, surrounded by vines and the rhythm of the seasons, assimilating our interrelationship with, and dependence on, nature. Alex and Alison got along well as brother and sister.

Their complementary strengths would be a double-edged sword. Could they work well together, especially if I weren't there?

Then one day, as I was driving up to the winery, it hit me that now was exactly the right time for me to start letting go. There was a reason I felt fatigued. The vision I had created in 1998 had run its course. I had pulled Sokol Blosser out of its financial abyss and done what was necessary to produce higher-quality wine: replanted the vineyards and taken them organic, brought in a winemaker with significant talent and expertise, upgraded winery equipment, built a new barrel cellar, and made sustainability a part of our mission. We were well poised for the future. I had completed what I wanted to do.

We were ready for a new vision, but I knew I wasn't the one to create it. The new vision would have to come from Alex and Alison, and they had to feel it deep inside in order to have the stamina to make it happen. I went for help to an old friend, Pat Frishkoff. Pat had developed the Family Business Program at Oregon State University. She was retired but still consulting and was willing to work with us. We started meeting.

I knew we could put a plan in place for a smooth transition. But then my kids would be on their own. They would face new challenges, different from mine. The growing number of new wineries, the flood of wine from foreign countries, the increasing consolidation of wineries into global companies, and the consolidation of wholesalers—all were changing the face of the wine business. An already competitive industry had grown more so. But they would have new opportunities as well. As more states dropped their barriers against winery-direct shipment to customers, that market would explode. As the global community grew closer, the possibilities for exporting would grow larger. As the Oregon wine industry expanded, more tourists would arrive. And who knew what changes the Internet would bring as it evolved?

Walking with Alex and Alison in the vineyard, summer 2005. Alex's dog, Andre, succeeded Muffin and Bagel as the vineyard dog. (Photo by Doreen L. Wynja.)

The vineyards, and later the winery, had absorbed me since I was in my twenties. They had brought me to maturity, and my whole sense of self was tied up with Sokol Blosser. I had devoted my life to making it work. In fact, it was my life. I began to recognize the challenges that lay ahead. First, I needed to find the best way to mentor my kids, pass control of the business to them, and let them have the thrill of taking Sokol Blosser forward. It would be difficult to give up control, but I thought I could. I was ready. The second challenge would be more difficult; it had to do with reshaping my own life. I had focused on business for most of my adulthood, eschewing vacations and seldom taking time to do anything just for fun.

Was it too late for me to learn to play? I headed out to the vineyard to walk among the vines and think about where to start.

———— ⁂ ————

Reflections

I wanted my story, and the story of Sokol Blosser, to unfold for you, the reader, as it happened, as I experienced it. I wanted you to smell the rich red dirt, hear the clatter of picking shears cutting clusters during harvest, and see the swallows swirling above the vines and diving for insects. I wanted you to feel the momentum as wine production in Oregon grew from a handful of couples into an internationally respected industry. And I wanted you to experience the challenges Bill and I faced as we established and developed Sokol Blosser.

To capture the flavor of the moment and keep the story moving forward, I withheld my reflections and analysis. But they are pressing to be expressed, and I am allowing them out on three topics: being a woman in business, what it means to own your own business, and why I think Sokol Blosser succeeded against all odds. Here goes . . .

As a woman navigating the mostly male world of agriculture and business, I never wished to be anything other than female. Sitting in meetings where I was the only woman and the conversation started with sports scores, I never wished I were a guy so I could really be part of the group. But I was acutely aware that being female came with a particular set of challenges, and I struggled with emotional issues of combining career and family that my male counterparts didn't. It was a period when roles were being redefined, and I felt the confusion.

Life seemed simpler for my mother. I never for a minute wanted her life, centered on golf, bridge, and her women's clubs, but I envied her clear-cut view of the world. She was not continually bothered by the questions that haunted me: Can I be both a good mother and a good businesswoman? Should I stay at home with my children or follow my desire to make my mark in the world? These questions created an undercurrent of discomfort and guilt with every choice I made. Whatever I did, I paid a price. But I wanted it all, kids and career, and I refused to sacrifice either.

My mother, born in 1905, accepted her role as society defined it: women stayed at home; men went to work. While I was growing up, the only friends of hers who worked were women whose families had fallen on hard times. They found genteel jobs, like clerking at an expensive women's clothing store. My smart, sassy mother had had a flourishing musical career before she married, at the advanced age of twenty-three. She was first violinist in the Chicago Women's Symphony, led a women's band, and was part of a women's string trio that played all over Chicago. She liked to boast that when she got married she was making more money than my father. She became pregnant six months after she married. When she was playing with her trio and someone in the audience asked, "Who's the fat one in the middle?" she knew her performing career was over. I never saw her play the violin, although she kept it and her stacks of music through five house moves. I had a publicity photo of her band enlarged as a gift—eleven women in their twenties looking carefree and snappy with their marcelled hair and flapper dresses—and it hung on her living room wall as a conversation piece. She may have chafed inside, but she never questioned society's expectations.

My friends and I wanted something different from our mothers' "dead-end" lives, but old ways die hard. We were filled with guilt at being dissatisfied with motherhood and felt selfish because we wanted personal fulfillment in a career. There were still enough women staying home with

My mother, Phyllis Sokol (in the foreground, fifth from the left), organized and led one of the first all-girl bands in the 1920s. They played at ballroom dances and at prominent events such as the trotting races in Kentucky. This publicity photo was taken in 1928.

their kids that working mothers suffered implied, if not outright, criticism. Once, when I had to leave for business, Alex wailed, "Why can't you be a real mother, like Wilma?" I looked at him blankly. It took me a minute to realize that he meant Wilma Flintstone, the prehistoric television cartoon wife whose life was her husband, kids, and shopping. I gave my sad little son a big hug, but then I left. I rationalized that it was the quality, not the quantity, of time I spent with my kids that mattered, and I tried to play with and pay attention to them, individually and together, while I was home.

Compromise was my way of dealing with all the demands. Work, kids, husband, relatives, friends, community activities, home upkeep, pets, garden—the list went on and on. I spent the years my kids were growing up feeling as if everyone had their hand out for a little piece of me. I never had enough time, and I shortchanged everything, but I wasn't willing to give up any of it. Somehow, I navigated through, and I still believe it is possible to have both kids and career. You just have to be willing to pare back everything you can, put up with the guilt, and be tired all the time—and you have to love what you're doing.

My generation, male and female, in college in the 1960s, went head-to-head with the establishment on civil rights, the Vietnam War, and women's rights. Questioning everything, we were eager to speak out and stand up for our beliefs. College friends were freedom riders in Mississippi and antiwar demonstrators. Bill and I took part in the antiwar March on Washington, which seemed to manifest the spirit of that decade—well organized, pacifist, and spiritually uplifting for the participants.

The feminist component of the 1960s antiestablishment movement was more complicated. We were determined to go where we weren't "allowed," and we were moderately successful. We started with obvious inequities, like dorm rules that restricted only women, and organizations, like Rotary, that didn't allow female members. I was one of the two first female members of the McMinnville Sunrise Rotary Club, and it seemed like an important victory at the time. But knocking down traditions just got us through the door. Then what? We had to redefine our roles as we went along. First, we tried to be just like the guys and fit into their corporate culture. Then we discovered that the male world wasn't as satisfying as we had hoped. I liked many of my fellow Rotarians, but I didn't really like Rotary. I quit after a few years.

Of my contemporaries who succeeded in business, a few got there by taking over for a husband who had run the family business and died suddenly. But most started out in one of the three professions traditionally open to women—teacher, social worker, nurse—and made it to the top by way of curious and convoluted paths. A few started as secretaries, learned the ropes, and jumped in when opportunity arose. Every time I have been on a businesswomen's panel with women my age or older, I have been amazed to hear their stories. Not one of them had business training in their fields of achievement. Once I sat next to an older woman who was the newly elected commissioner from Lincoln County. She had started out as a secretary and had worked in the county office for years before running for office. When I jokingly asked her how long it had taken her to realize she could do the job better than the men for whom she worked, she laughed, and then replied in total seriousness: "Two weeks."

Today, young women who want to get ahead can aim straight at their goal. The doors are open for Alison's generation. My generation bears scars from blasting through them. In the male-dominated wine business, my friends and I developed an old girls' network. If I had a question about which distributor to choose in a certain market or about a particular person in the industry, I could go to battle-savvy, successful women like Eugenia Keegan, Margaret Duckhorn, Jeanne Davis, and Laurie Puzo for advice. We didn't see one another very often, but I knew I could call them anytime, and they were unfailingly helpful.

Surprisingly, it took years for us to realize that we didn't really want the kind of equality we had been fighting for. We didn't want to be just like men. We looked at the world differently, managed differently, thought differently than men. And that wasn't bad. In fact, it added positive elements to the mix. The realization that men and women have different strengths has made business more creative and competitive and resulted in new models for success. But women can succeed only if the men currently at the top understand the benefits of sharing power. Women who have dis-

Eugenia Keegan, Margaret Duckhorn, and I at Portland's Classic Wines Auction in 1993, the year I was honorary chairperson.

covered they couldn't rise within the traditional business structure have left in droves to start their own companies. But being a company owner has challenges of its own.

⋮

The yin and yang of owning your own business are that you have both the exhilaration of power and control and the weight of total responsibility for your organization's welfare and success. Looking in from the outside, people have no idea. When I participated on a panel of female business owners before a group of Portland State University's MBA students, one young woman said she liked the idea of owning her own business because then she could take time off from work whenever she wanted. She was joking, right? No, she was serious. We explained that while you were theoretically free to take off, in reality you were tied down by responsibility. Being a business owner meant working more hours, not less.

Working for yourself means you cannot escape emotionally, even when you are physically distant. Your business is always on your mind. Every problem is your problem; the business rises or falls on the decisions you make. You hire employees to help, but you take the responsibility for their performance. If they screw up, you suffer the consequences.

That exhilarating sense of power? It comes with ties that bind. My ideas about what works come from experience, not theory, but I am aware of business models and I've toyed with business diagrams. I never liked the traditional pyramid, with the president at the top and rows of managers and employees below. It doesn't reflect the way the president depends on the employees. For a while, I liked the concept of the company as a circle, with the president in the middle and the various segments of the business fanning out in wedges. It gave production, sales, and accounting their own portions of the whole, and it showed that if one part of the business didn't do its job, it broke the circle and weakened the whole. As president, it put me in the thick of things, the axis on which the wheel turned.

But neither of these diagrams really captures what it feels like to own your own business. A more accurate model for small business would be the traditional pyramid turned upside down. The owner is kneeling at the bottom, supporting the rest of the operation and taking the punishment if any of it comes crashing down. The reality of owning your own business is that everything rests on your shoulders—Atlas holding up the world, not Jupiter looking down on his kingdom. Am I complaining? Not at all. Do I like owning my own business? Absolutely. I am more than willing to endure the stress, for the privilege of being the decision-maker.

∵∵

Sokol Blosser had such an improbable start. Bill and I were unlikely candidates for success: two liberal-arts graduates with no experience, planting a grape variety with a poor track record in a state with no wine industry. I am always asked how I got into the wine industry. What made us plant a vineyard, and in Oregon, and at a time when a wine industry barely existed? It's the obvious question, the first one. But I don't think it's the most interesting one. The real question is: how did we survive? People start wild, weird things every day. They usually don't last. We started a wild, weird thing that did. How can I explain that? Was it fate? Maybe some of it was. The obvious thing was our willingness to take risks. They were backed up by research and not all of them panned out, but we knew we had to take them. Beyond that, other factors contributed to our survival.

Think how technology and society changed during the last years of the twentieth century. Life was different when we started in the 1970s. Not simpler, really, but different. Words and phrases now part of everyday vocabulary didn't exist then. When we started farming, we talked about the environment but not about biodiversity, the soil foodweb, or sustainability. We didn't think to call ourselves entrepreneurs. E-mail, the Internet, cell phones, and laptop computers were not part of our vernacular or our arsenal of business tools. Now we use computer software for accounting, sales, marketing, wine production, and communication in ways that we couldn't have imagined thirty years ago. In every part of our operation, we continue to learn.

I sometimes view my years of running Sokol Blosser as making a series of choices that, once made, simply created new messes to deal with. Conditions changed, new information surfaced. Whatever I did, whatever I decided, I always knew there would be mopping up somewhere. We always had to be willing and able to move quickly, shift gears, grab new opportunities, and redo things that weren't working.

Overall, the last quarter of the twentieth century saw the wine industry boom throughout the world. We started out thinking that what we were doing in Oregon was unique, and later realized we were part of a global wine-industry expansion. While we were starting our project in Oregon, others were doing the same thing in Italy, Australia, New Zealand, Austria, Argentina, and Chile, as well as in all fifty states. Oregon has been on the cusp of global growth in the wine industry and has, within one generation, become an internationally acclaimed producer of great wine. I am proud to have been part of that.

In popular image, the winegrower leads the good life at a leisurely pace. In truth, wine is a fast-moving, competitive business, made even more so by the flood of new wineries, both domestic and foreign. Enter any wine store, and you will be confronted with hundreds of different wines from which to choose. Restaurant wine lists contain so many wines that they can be read like books and measured in inches. Most people buy only one bottle at a time, so much of the wine just sits waiting for customers. Meanwhile, behind the scenes, wineries are vying to get their bottles onto the shelves and onto the lists. For every wine in a shop or on a restaurant list, there are dozens of others that didn't make it. As the market for Oregon wine has increased, so has the competition. Placing Sokol Blosser wine in the best wine shops and restaurants, and then keeping it there, has required constant attention.

⋮⋮

Continual learning, adaptability, luck, and willingness to compete have helped Sokol Blosser survive. But I think there is more to the story. I can reduce our survival and success to one word: *determination*. Giving up, calling it quits? No way. I resolved I would succeed. The challenge, the excitement, and the satisfaction have been in clearing the hurdles, maneuvering past the obstacles, and finding the best route.

As a teenager, I read Albert Camus's *Myth of Sisyphus* and couldn't understand how Camus could call Sisyphus a happy man. All he did was roll a stone up a hill. Now, many years later, I understand. It is the journey, not the end, that gives meaning. And if the journey is made with the heart as well as the head, with as much respect for the planet as for profit, so much the better.

⸻ ⋮⋮ ⸻

An Annotated Time Line
of the Oregon Wine Industry

Oregon's short wine industry history is full of events not fully covered in my narrative. A complete history of the development of Oregon wine would cover many more people and events.

1961   Richard Sommer planted Oregon's first post-Prohibition vinifera grapes, in the Umpqua Valley near Roseburg.

1966   David and Diana Lett bought their Dundee Hills property and spent their honeymoon getting it ready for planting the first post-Prohibition Willamette Valley vinifera vineyard. They had rooted the grape plants the previous year in Corvallis.

1970   Oregon had five bonded wineries and thirty-five acres of planted vinifera vineyard.

1972   Oregon's landmark land-use legislation mandated statewide land-use planning. Winegrowers worked at the county level to preserve hillsides for agriculture that otherwise would have been designated as residential "view property."

1976   Matt Kramer started his writing career as a food writer, restaurant reviewer, and wine writer for *Willamette Week,* Portland's alternative weekly newspaper. He went on to write definitive studies of major wine regions and became a columnist for *The Wine Spectator,* but maintained Portland as his home base.

1977   The Oregon Liquor Control Commission adopted new labeling regulations for wine, after both northern and southern Oregon wineries negotiated a proposal on which they agreed.

Acting on a request from the wine industry, Oregon's legislature created the Table Wine Research Advisory Board (TWRAB), funded by a tax on wine grapes. Its mission was to promote enological and viticultural research. Funds were funneled through Oregon State University, which started to conduct research on trellising, cover crops, crop estimating, crop loads, rootstock, clones, malolactic cultures, and acid reduction. In 1983, TWRAB was modified to become the Wine Advisory Board (WAB), and its mission was expanded to include promotion of Oregon wines as well as research. Funding for WAB came from a tonnage assessment, to be shared equally between growers and wineries and from a tax of two cents per gallon on all nonexempt wine sold in the state. To protect small wineries, including the whole Oregon industry, wineries under a certain size were exempted from the latter tax.

1978   The Willamette Valley's Winegrowers Council of Oregon (WCO) and southern Oregon's Oregon Wine Growers Association (OWGA) joined to form the first statewide organization, the Oregon Winegrowers Association (OWA). The joint venture of these two long-standing organizations served an important education and communication function and allowed the wine industry to act with one voice in the legislative arena.

The first "Discover Oregon Wines" brochure guided tourists to wineries.

1979   The Steamboat Conference, an annual gathering of international Pinot Noir winemakers at the Steamboat Inn on the North Umpqua River in southern Oregon, had its inaugural meeting. The three-day event—focused on technical tastings and honest and open discussion of Pinot Noir production—was the brainchild of Stephen Cary from Oregon and Mike Richmond from California and started out with just Oregon and California winemakers.

Gault-Millau, France's innovative food and wine magazine, held a wine-tasting *olympiade* in which The Eyrie Vineyard's 1975 South Block Pinot Noir placed in the top ten in the Pinot Noir category, giving Oregon its first international recognition. Robert Drouhin felt that Burgundy had not been fairly represented and staged a rematch in early 1980; there Eyrie's same wine placed second to a 1959 Musigny. The *New York Times* picked up the story, and interest in Oregon wine surged.

1980   There were thirty-four bonded wineries in Oregon with 1,238 acres of planted vineyard.

1983   Stephen Cary and Reuben Rich established Cary Oregon Wines to market a group of Oregon wineries in the national market. Before this time, only a very few Oregon wineries had marketed nationally.

The first *Oregon Winegrape Grower's Guide,* a compendium of articles by winegrowers to help newcomers get started, was published by the Oregon Winegrowers Association. Marilyn Webb was the editor.

The Oregon Wine Advisory Board was established with the dual missions of research and marketing.

1984   Elaine Cohen and Rich Hopkins started the *Oregon Wine Press,* a monthly newspaper, to publicize Oregon wineries and tourism. Free to the public, the paper started with a circulation of three hundred and grew to twenty thousand copies in distribution.

Willamette Valley went on wine labels as Oregon's new American Viticultural Area (AVA). The proposal was written by David Adelsheim.

Oregon hosted the first International Cool Climate Viticulture Symposium, organized through Oregon State University. Prominent new- and old-world vinifera researchers and producers attended and gave talks.

1985   Oregon Pinot Noir outshone French at the Burgundy Challenge at the International Wine Center in New York, in which Pinot Noirs from the 1983 vintage in Oregon and Burgundy were tasted against each other.

1987   The International Pinot Noir Celebration debuted in McMinnville.

Robert Drouhin purchased land in the Dundee Hills to start his Oregon vineyard.

1988   Governor Neil Goldschmidt led a group of Oregon winemakers on a good-will mission to Burgundy, France.

Willamette Valley Vineyards, led by Jim Bernau, made the first public offering of stock in an Oregon winery. The approach of selling small amounts of affordable stock enabled thousands of wine-loving consumers to consider themselves winery owners. In 1994 the stock was listed on the NASDAQ.

1989   Pinot Noir: America, a collaboration of California and Oregon Pinot Noir producers, began its series of trade tastings around the country. This cooperative effort, spearheaded by Josh Jensen from Calera Winery in California, represented a recognition that the real competition was not between California and Oregon Pinot Noir but between Pinot Noir and Cabernet Sauvignon. The group focused its efforts on popularizing Pinot Noir among chefs and sommeliers.

1990   Trappist Abbey in Lafayette opened the Abbey Wine Warehouse with six winery customers, beginning an important service to Willamette Valley wineries.

Federal funding under a Marketing Assistance Program provided funds for Oregon and Washington wineries to do joint marketing efforts in the export arena.

Phylloxera was identified for the first time in Willamette Valley vinifera vineyards.

There were seventy-four bonded Oregon wineries and 6,050 vineyard acres.

1991   The fourth edition of the *Oregon Winegrape Grower's Guide,* edited by Ted Casteel, was published by the Oregon Winegrowers Association.

The Hotel Vintage Plaza opened in downtown Portland. Part of the Kimpton Group of small luxury hotels, the Vintage Plaza sported an Oregon wine theme, with each of the suites named for an Oregon winery.

1992   The Oregon Chapter of Women for WineSense was formed, spearheaded by Helen Dusschee, Karen Hinsdale, Maria Ponzi, Elaine Cohen and Susan Sokol Blosser.

The first *¡Salud!* Barrel Auction was held, in which thirty wineries each

donated half a barrel of Pinot Noir to raise money for health-care services for vineyard workers. This ambitious project started organizing in
1990 and was made a reality by a small group of winery people and local
doctors, especially Nancy Ponzi from Ponzi Vineyards, Steve Vuylsteke
from Oak Knoll Winery, and Dr. Larry Hornick, a radiologist active with
the Tuality Health Care Foundation.

1994   Oregon Wine Marketing Coalition, a cooperative marketing group,
started its program of Oregon wine tastings and education around the
country, targeting both the trade and consumers.

1996   Salmon-Safe, an environmental marketing program, was started by the
Pacific Rivers Council and directed by Dan Kent.

1997   Low Input Viticulture & Enology (LIVE) program started in Oregon as a
way to set standards for sustainable agricultural practices.

2000   There were 132 bonded Oregon wineries with 11,100 acres of vineyard.

The first Oregon Pinot Camp, a program organized by forty wineries to
bring key wine buyers to experience Oregon wine country, was held.

2001   The LIVE program received international certification by the International
Office of Biological Control, making it the first of many sustainable agricultural programs in the United States to receive international certification.

2002   The first U.S. Green Building Council LEED (Leadership in Energy and
Environmental Design) certification for a winery building was awarded
to Sokol Blosser for its barrel cellar.

2003   The fifth edition of the *Oregon Grape Grower's Guide,* now titled *Oregon Viticulture,* was released. It was published by Oregon State University Press
and edited by Ed Hellman.

2004   The Northwest Viticulture Center opened at Chemeketa Community College in Salem, offering hands-on instruction in winemaking and vineyard
work.

The WAB was replaced by the newly configured Oregon Wine Board—
with the same funding as WAB but no longer under the auspices of the
Department of Agriculture.

2005   The first three of six proposed new AVAs went into effect—Dundee Hills, Yamhill-Carlton District, and McMinnville.

Oregon's wine industry ranked second in the United States for number of wineries and fourth for amount of wine produced.

There were 350 wineries in Oregon and 14,000 acres of vineyard.

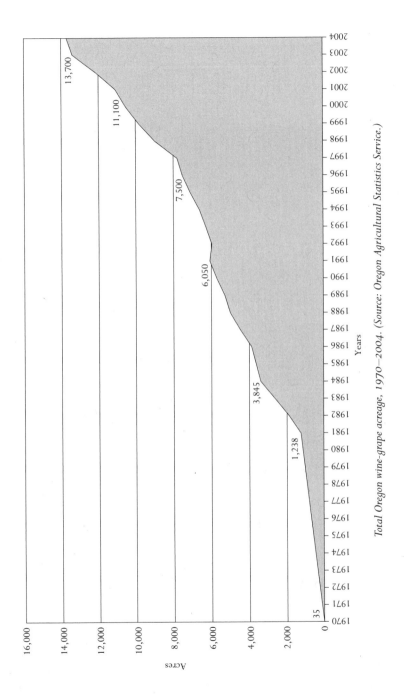

Total Oregon wine-grape acreage, 1970–2004. (Source: Oregon Agricultural Statistics Service.)

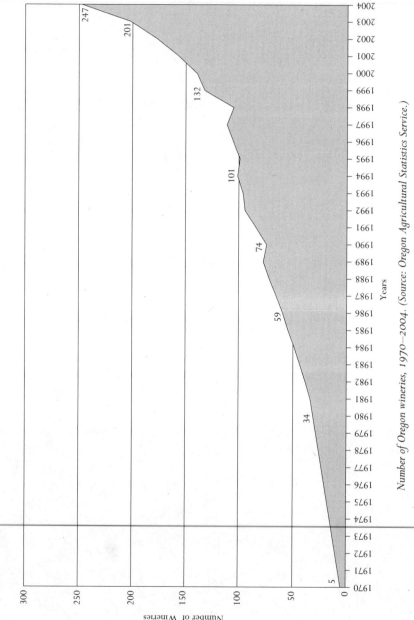

Number of Oregon wineries, 1970–2004. (Source: Oregon Agricultural Statistics Service.)

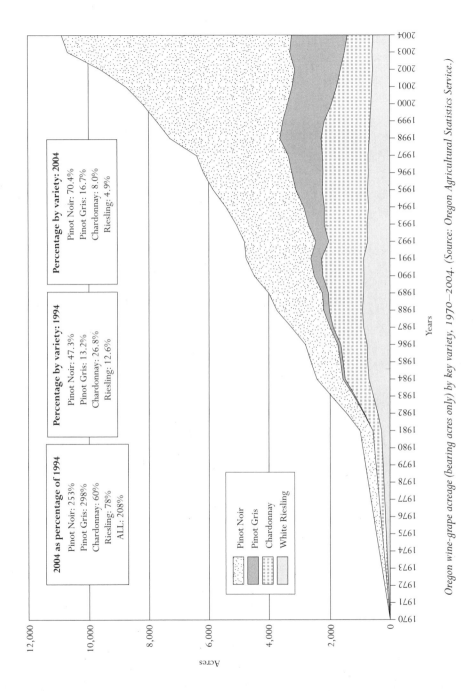

2004 as percentage of 1994
Pinot Noir: 253%
Pinot Gris: 298%
Chardonnay: 60%
Riesling: 78%
ALL: 208%

Percentage by variety: 1994
Pinot Noir: 47.3%
Pinot Gris: 13.2%
Chardonnay: 26.8%
Riesling: 12.6%

Percentage by variety: 2004
Pinot Noir: 70.4%
Pinot Gris: 16.7%
Chardonnay: 8.0%
Riesling: 4.9%

Pinot Noir
Pinot Gris
Chardonnay
White Riesling

Acres

12,000

10,000

8,000

6,000

4,000

2,000

0

1970 1971 1972 1973 1974 1975 1976 1977 1978 1979 1980 1981 1982 1983 1984 1985 1986 1987 1988 1989 1990 1991 1992 1993 1994 1995 1996 1997 1998 1999 2000 2001 2002 2003 2004

Years

Oregon wine-grape acreage (bearing acres only) by key variety, 1970–2004. (Source: Oregon Agricultural Statistics Service.)

INDEX

Text: 11/15 Perpetua
Display: Perpetua
Designer: Sandy Drooker
Cartographer: James Sinclair
Compositor: Integrated Composition Systems
Printer and Binder: Thomson-Shore, Inc.